The Fisherman's Gospel Manual

GRAHAM MAIR

CHAPTER TWO
Plumstead, London SE18 3AF

First published in 1994
by Chapter Two

Bible quotations from the King James Version (KJV),
New Translation of J.N. Darby.

ISBN 1 85307 041 6

British Library Cataloguing in Publication Data
A catalogue record for this book is available
from the British Library.

Designed and produced in England for
Chapter Two, 13 Plum Lane, London, SE18 3AF by
Nuprint Ltd., Station Road, Harpenden, Herts. AL5 4SE

'To him who loves us, and has washed us from our sins in his blood.... To him be the glory ... to the ages of ages.'

Revelation 1, J.N. Darby Translation

Correspondence with troubled souls welcomed at the addresses below.

Are you engaged in spreading the gospel and using this book? Write to me for our SPECIAL OFFER for active literature distributors:

Graham Mair
'Inchmore'
10 Haig Street
Portknockie
Buckie
AB56 2NT.
Telephone (0542) 840596

If you would like a free New Testament, contact me at the above address or write to:

Bible Distributors
13 Plum Lane
LONDON
SE18 3AF.

Contents

Foreword 9

Introduction 11

1 He is Not a Disappointment 13
2 The Happy Skipper 15
3 The Buckie Disaster 18
4 Which Harbour? 20
5 The Happiest Moment of my Life 22
6 Which Light is Flashing—Red or Green? 25
7 The Fisherman's Hymn 27
8 Peace 28
9 A Voice from the Deep 29
10 Distress Channel 33
11 My Experience and Conversion 35
12 Lighthouses 39
13 Psalm 23—Fisherman's Version 40
14 Setting the Course 41
15 Old Sea Dog's Last Call 43
16 A Friend at All Times 46
17 Lifeline 48
18 John Noble Stephen: Lost at Sea 49
19 Shipping Forecasts 52
20 On Course to Jesus 54
21 Hymn 58
22 Whither Bound? 59
23 The Seaman's Prayer 63
24 Heaven's Lifeboat 64
25 Calvary 67
26 The Fisher Lad's Last Song 68
27 'His Way is in the Sea' 70
28 The Message 72
29 The Fisherman's Perfect Cure 74
30 Danger 76

31	Personal Testimony	78
32	A Tale of the Sea	81
33	I Won't Have to Cross Jordan Alone	84
34	Jesus Called and I was Ready	86
35	The Master of the Sea	88
36	Safe into Harbour	89
37	'Haven of Rest'	90
38	A New Life	92
39	The Fisherman's Change	93
40	The Gospel Ship	95
41	All is Well	98
42	Love that Changed Me	103
43	Will Your Anchor Hold?	105
44	Under the Wave	107
45	'Nothing Shall be Impossible With God'	110
46	My Pilot	112
47	Barometer	113
48	'He Maketh the Storm a Calm'	115
49	'For God Speaketh Once, Yea Twice'	116
50	Lie by till Morning	118
51	Saviour, Pilot Me	119
52	Bill Duthie	120
53	Harbour Bell	122
54	The Controller of the Sea	123
55	Safe Keeping	124
56	The Gospel Compass	126
57	In Jesus I'm Safe Evermore	128
58	After Many Days	129
59	The Best of Intentions	133
60	Security	134
61	'Ready Now!'	136
62	Saved at the End	139
63	Miraculous Deliverance	141
64	What a Saviour we have Found	148
65	Psalm 23	150
66	Almost Saved	152
67	The Story of the 'Shegress'	154

68	Psalm 107	156
69	Saved from a Watery Grave	158
70	Fishers of Men	160
71	Distress Message	161
72	Accidentally Lost at Sea	163
73	Great Joy	165
74	Homeward Bound	167
75	Till We Meet Again	168
76	How A Skipper was Saved after many Days	169
77	Watching from the Shore	172
78	Saved in a Remarkable Place	174
79	Lifeboat Refused	176
80	Wonderful Change	178
81	He was Drowned; I was Saved	181
82	Hymn II	183
83	The Lord is Coming	184
84	Testimony	186
85	What Makes a Man Ready to Die?	191

Acknowledgements

I would like to take this opportunity to thank all those who were involved in the contribution of material for this book and also those who have given support and encouragement to me whilst I have been compiling the book.

I would especially like to thank George Wilson for drawing and painting the front cover and sketches; also thanks to David Eastwood and Alan Burnett-Leys for the sketches they did; and also Jenny Mair for the many hours she spent editing and typing all the articles.

Foreword

Dear Reader,

My desire in compiling this book is that through reading it *you*, if you are not yet saved, *you* may be led to know the Lord Jesus as your own personal Saviour and know the joy of having your sins forgiven and a hope beyond death. If you are a believer in our Lord Jesus Christ, may you be here as a true ambassador of Christ in this dark and dreary world, 'Let your light so shine before men' (Matthew 5:16).

For those who go down to the sea in ships, that do business in great waters, the sea is a job with many dangers, and that is why it is so important to be ready to die. How many fishermen have lost their lives at sea? Many a fisherman has left home, never to return, sailed from the harbour for the last time, not knowing that his voyage was a **Voyage to Eternity**.

As a fisherman I know the way of life and the dangers attached to it. Fishing is a way of life with a lot of time spent away from home. You cannot really understand the life unless you have been a fisherman yourself.

When I left school to become a fisherman, I had already accepted the Lord Jesus as my Saviour some time before. But as the years went by I had lost the joy of my salvation...and the latter years of school life had been wasted. Some of the things I did I would be ashamed to write about.

I left school and started looking for a berth aboard a fishing boat. At that stage in my Christian life I was like a ship drifting without a rudder; I wasn't worried about what kind of boat I went on; whether the crew were Christians or not, I didn't care. After a few odd trips here and there I got the chance to go away on a Buckie boat for a couple of trips, so accepted.

We left Peterhead on the Thursday night for the Norwegian grounds which were about a hundred and fifty miles away and I knew that the trip could last anything from seven to nine days. I was quite pleased we would be away from home on Sunday as that would mean I would miss going to the meetings and miss the gospel preaching: something I had wanted to do for a while.

As we were steaming off I thought back to my conversion and my Christian upbringing, and I knew that God was speaking to me. We arrived at the fishing grounds on Friday morning and started fishing. As we were clearing the first haul of fish, God was still speaking to me. I looked around and saw that all the crew were on deck so I made my way down to the cabin, still with my oil-skins on, and I prayed to the Lord Jesus for the first time in many years to restore me. I took the Lord Jesus to be my pilot again. On the next haul we broke down so we headed back for Peterhead on the Saturday night. The next night there I was sitting listening to God's word being preached, but for the first time in years I was pleased to be there. Since that time the Christian path has grown ever brighter.

A few weeks later I got a job on a Portknockie boat, the 'Courier', which was skippered by a Christian friend working out of Kinlochbervie. Not only did they help me to learn the job, but there were those who cared for my Christian life. The Lord was looking after me and was piloting me through life.

A year later, my father bought his own boat 'Venture' and we have often proved God's hand in circumstances. Fishing is facing uncertain times, but as believers we are not promised an easy path. We are, however, promised that the Lord will be with us in all our circumstances.

All the stories in this book are true and are a witness to the saving power of God in many adverse circumstances. I trust that you will enjoy reading them and that they will be of help to you.

Graham Mair

Introduction

Rescue Mission

I WANT TO BEGIN this book by telling you of the greatest rescue mission that has ever taken place. You may have been rescued at sea or you've no doubt read of how brave men on lifeboats and in helicopters have risked their lives for others. You could fill a book with these stories.

The beginning of the greatest ever rescue mission was when God in His love for sinners gave His only begotten son: 'THE FATHER HAS SENT THE SON AS SAVIOUR OF THE WORLD' (1 John 4:14). The rescue mission had begun. You may be asking, 'Why do I need to be rescued? Why do I need to be saved?' Because you are a sinner: 'FOR ALL HAVE SINNED' (Romans 3:23).

The Lord Jesus came here into this world, born in a stable and lived a perfect life: 'WHO DID NO SIN, NEITHER WAS GUILE FOUND IN HIS MOUTH' (1 Peter 2:22); yet He was crucified and died on a cross. 'Why did He have to die?' you may be asking. 'Christ died for our sins', and shed His precious blood and rose from amongst the dead: 'He was buried and that he was raised the third day' (1 Corinthians 15:4) and He now **lives** in heaven, a glorious Saviour. 'I became dead, and behold, I am living to the ages of ages' (Revelation 1:18).

What love He showed to rescue us from hell! Great and heroic rescues, involving suffering and self-sacrifice have been borne by many; many have given their lives for others. The supreme sacrifice of Jesus, who gave Himself for our sins, must alone ever stand as the means by which storm tossed mariners on the sea of life can be rescued from peril and brought by Him into the harbour of peace.

I trust that by the end of this book you will have asked

11

the Lord Jesus into your life and then your name will be written in heaven in the Lamb's book of Life—**another rescued sinner**.

GRAHAM MAIR

1

He is Not a Disappointment

L EAVING SCHOOL AT SIXTEEN and beginning a career at sea aboard the fishing vessel, St. Kilda INS 47, I had little thought of God. Having in past years been faithful to a Sunday school and Bible class I thought I had 'attained' or even 'inherited' what God required of me. After attaining many things in the world, things which in many peoples' lives take the place of God, I found for myself they had no real, lasting satisfaction.

When I was seventeen, a caring aunt suggested that I accompany her to gospel meetings in Hopeman Baptist church, in a small fishing village on the NorthEast coast. My vain thoughts of an angry, pitiless and uncaring God were soon put to flight as I heard of the loving, merciful and caring Saviour of Calvary, Jesus Christ, God's own Son.

Not long after I began attending the gospel meetings I began to feel that the message of the gospel required a response; until then all I had done was reject God's salvation...but there was now a growing conviction in my heart and soul and it seemed to have a voice of its own, it warned 'Get right with God!'

At the height of my conviction in November 1989 I left for sea one Sunday night with one question, 'Where will I go when I die?' I knew full well the answer, 'Hell' and it would be my own fault. On Saturday 25th November 1989 the burden of my sin was too much to bear, so as I was going about my work aboard the boat I made the break and I decided (amid all the lies the Devil tried to tell me) to

13

get saved. I took off my oilskins, washed and dried my hands and went down to the cabin and confessed it all to God; I then asked Jesus to be my Saviour and Lord and to live forever in my heart. On getting down on my knees, I knew I'd been born again!

Keeping good fellowship and company with believers I soon went on as a young Christian, never looking back. I praise God for a full salvation, a life free from the power of sin and death. I began to preach the gospel in 1990 and today am still involved with the proclamation of the Glad Tidings.

For me salvation came thirty-five miles NorthWest off the Butt of Lewis; you can turn and trust Him now. Believe on His work and His name and you'll be able to agree with the hymn writer, 'He is Not a Disappointment!'

Brian R. More

2

The Happy Skipper

SOME YEARS AGO there lived a good Christian fisherman in the village of St. Monance, on the coast of Fife in Scotland. His name was Andrew Davidson, and he was owner and skipper of the fishing boat called the 'Rose in June'. The herring season came, and Andrew Davidson and his little crew prepared to go to sea. He had but lately been married, and before leaving home he knelt down with his young wife, and asked God to keep her safely while he was away; but he had not said a word about his own safety and her heart sank within her at the thought. The night after the 'Rose in June' sailed with a fleet of other vessels, a terrible storm raged all along the coast. Early next morning, a crowd of women and children, made up of the families of the absent fishermen, gathered on the beach. Every eye was strained across the waters, to catch the first glimpse of the returning boats. One by one they struggled in; shouts of joy and thankfulness arose from one and another, as a husband, a father, a son, or a brother sprang ashore, but the 'Rose in June' did not come. Driven by the storm and dashed upon the rocks, she became a total wreck. Turned bottom upwards, her crew of six men clung to her keel with desperate energy. No other boat was near to help or save them and all around them the wild waves were rolling and roaring, threatening every moment to tear each man from his hold and dash him to pieces on the sharp rocks. Andrew Davidson thought of **JESUS** in that hour of need and peril, and in the face of certain death, that thought did more for him that anything else in the world—it made him happy. It may be that he remembered then how Paul and Silas glorified God in the prison of Philippi; for he shouted, loud and clear above the storm: 'Now boys, let us sing a hymn of praise to God, and at once began to sing this verse:

> My Jesus, I love Thee, I know Thou art mine;
> For Thee all the pleasures of sin I resign;
> My gracious Redeeemer, my Saviour art Thou;
> If ever I loved Thee, my Jesus 'tis now.

These were his last words. He had hardly finished the verse, when a huge wave dashed over him with great force and in an instant he was swept away 'from every stormy wind that blows', into the haven of eternal rest. A sad silence fell upon the men who had been trying to join in that hymn of praise. For a while no one spoke. At last, John Allan, the mate of the little vessel, who was also a believer in Jesus, exclaimed, 'Come my lads, let us go on with that hymn that our skipper is finishing in heaven'. And these brave men, rocking on their wrecked boat with the waves dashing and the wild winds wailing around them, sang on till they had finished the hymn:

> I will love Thee in life, I will love Thee in death,
> And praise Thee as long as Thou lendest me breath;
> And say when the death-dew lies cold on my brow;
> If ever I loved Thee, my **Jesus**, 'tis now.

Just as they were finishing the hymn another huge wave burst over the boat and carried the young mate away to join his skipper, friend and shipmate in that blessed world

> Where anchored safe his weary soul shall find eternal rest,
> And not a wave of trouble roll across his peaceful breast.

The rest of the crew of that wrecked boat escaped with

their lives, but they never forgot the scene they had witnessed during that terrible storm, and no sermon ever preached about the preciousness of **JESUS** could ever make an impression on them as was made by that memorable scene. They felt deep down in their very souls, that the truth in **JESUS** is the best of all truth, because it satisfies and makes us happy.

W. Chalmers
Portknockie

3

The Buckie Disaster

COME YOUNG AND OLD, both great and small, come
   listen unto me;
Come listen to me and you shall hear a story of the sea;
A gallant boat and crew one night to the sea became
   prey,
So that night it was their last night on earth—that night
   in Buckie Bay.

Eight all told of seamen bold, including two little boys,
While leaving home they did not think it would be their
   last goodbye,
Their time was come, their race was run, no longer here
   to roam,
So that noble crew they perished there, in sight of land
   and home.

Oh! think of that noble crew that night, when struggling
   for their lives,
Away from home and parents dear, from children and
   from wives,
They fought midst storm and wind and tide against a
   westerly gale,
But every signal seemed to fail for help was of no avail.

Twas on the 13th February, in the year of 1920,
A storm did rage the Moray Firth, the night was dark and
   dreary,
The gallant boat was nearing home, in the darkness met
   her fate,

She struck the rocks, and foundered—and help came just
   too late.

Though willing hands stood on the shore, witnessing the
   scene,
Their very hearts were like to break, though help they
   could not give
The mother gazed upon her son, and with most anxious
   care
A prayer went up to God above, to help those in despair.

The lifeboat reached, we all regret, just then to be late,
Meanwhile the men were sinking fast, death stared them
   in the face;
The men kept clinging to the wreck, believing help
   would come,
Then hopelessly they disappeared, death caught them
   one by one.

Oh brother dear, a warning take, all ye who plough the
   sea,
Of this sad news and see that you in Christ you fall asleep;
The message left by them to thee, we think we hear them
   say:
'Prepare lest you should meet your fate, like them in
   Buckie Bay'.

The boat Loyal and crew no more shall plough the raging
   main,
No more on earth we'll see their face or call them by their
   name;
They're gone we hope where storms do cease for Jesus is
   the Way
But that night will be remembered long—that night in
   Buckie Bay.

4

Which Harbour?

S OON OUR FRAIL, weathered bark will reach our eternal harbour and sail life's seas no more. Death is an unavoidable appointment, 'As it is appointed unto men once to die, but after this the judgement' (Hebrews 9:27); and 'No one hath control over the day of death' (Ecclesiastes 8:8).

Life passes so quickly and for each one of us 'the sands of time are sinking', 'Now my days...are passed away as the swift ships' (Job 9:25,26). True of the youngest, true of the oldest and will be true of us all, for we soon shall reach the end of life's journey and sail into the harbour of our eternal destiny. 'How long shall thy journey be?' (Nehemiah 2:6). No one knows; it might be many years or just a few years.

I wonder which harbour we shall reach: heaven above where all is love or hell below where all is woe. We work out of Peterhead harbour and we come in and out as we like, but only after we've asked permission from the Control Tower and have been told that the way is clear. But when we reach the harbour of our eternal destiny there is no going out, 'For years few in number shall pass and I shall go the way whence I shall not return' (Job 16:22).

You see all kinds of boats passing you at sea and all bound for a destination, a destination which may be near or far but every throb of the engine brings it nearer its desired haven. Every breath you take, each heart beat is taking you nearer your final destination. We are all sailing over the sea of time and soon for all of us, we shall reach our final harbour. Which entrance are you making for?

'Broad is the way that leads to destruction...narrow is the way that leads to life' (Matthew 7:13,14).

Is it going to be HEAVEN with JESUS or HELL without Him?

G.M.

5

The Happiest Moment of my Life

ONE OF THE EARLIEST RECOLLECTIONS I have of an awakening to spiritual things was when at the age of six or seven some of the young boys whom I used to play with lined us up and would say: 'Willie Forman, you're saved; David John Forman, you're saved; Walter Brown, you're saved' and then it came my turn: 'Alex McLean, you're not saved.' It all seemed like a boyish thing, all to be forgotten by the rest in a few minutes, but to me these words were indelibly written in my heart. 'Alex McLean, you're not saved.' The war years were soon upon us and I gradually slipped further and further into the world of pleasure and sin.

One day when I came home my mother said to me, 'There is a man in to see you.' He wanted me to go to the winter fishing on the west coast of Scotland with him, to make up a crew. I gladly accepted so on the Monday morning I went down to rig out the ship. To my surprise the crew was mostly made up of Christians.

On the following Monday we set sail for the west coast. The weather was bad and most of the crew were seasick which is quite normal after being ashore for a while. Going along the north coast towards Cape Wrath, I was in the wheelhouse keeping watch—smoking a cigarette and steering, when into the wheelhouse came a young man of twenty-two, the same age as myself. His name was John Noble Stephen. He asked me if I was ever seasick, in answer I said, 'No it never bothers me.' Then he asked if I ever thought about my soul. 'Yes,' I said, 'I do'; and with that he said, 'That's a good sign.'

As the days passed he would quote a verse from the Bible and sometimes the verse of a hymn. I felt myself becoming increasingly interested in what he had to say. One night we were in Stornoway with poor weather, and John and his brother, Campbell, and their cousin, Alex Stephen, were on the pier; they asked if I would like to have a walk with them up the street. 'No No, it's all right I'll see you when you come back' (I was held back by financial embarrassment). John quickly said, 'Hey come on' so I ended up going.

I was so impressed by their manner of life; it was so different from mine. At the weekend the skipper gave us some money so I went off on my own. Coming back to the ship in the early hours of the next morning, John was waiting for me in the galley. All the others were asleep. I whispered to him, 'What are you doing here?'

'I'm waiting for you. Will you come with me to the gospel meeting tonight?' I explained that my clothes were not suitable—the suit I was wearing belonged to another man and the shoes were well down in the heel. John told me that no one would be looking at my clothes, so I decided to go.

That night I heard Mr Cecil Lawrence preach the gospel on the Scripture, 'Behold, I come quickly' (Revelation 22:12); how that the Lord Jesus was coming without warning. We sang a hymn at the end of the meeting.

> Blest Saviour in the Glory, who gave Thyself for me,
> I'm thine oh wondrous story, thine to eternity,
> And pleasures for a season, no longer joys afford,
> For lo I'm all enraptured with Christ my risen Lord.

John's brother, Campbell, asked if I would like to go to the preacher's house for tea, but I told them I was going back to the boat. On the way down, I stopped at the foot of

Church Street and began to reflect upon the life that I had led: What had the world done for me? I thought about all the pleasures of sin—the dance hall, the cinema, the public house, smoking etc. Then I thought, what about the other side?

Well, the preacher had spoken about a Man, who died upon the cross, the Lord Jesus Christ, God's Son. I said, 'I don't know how to pray, but I will trust Jesus Christ as my Saviour NOW!' There was no flashing light or voice, but there was a thought, 'What about tomorrow?' I said, 'I'll trust God for tomorrow' then quickly made for the ship.

The next morning after breakfast, the cook asked who would go up for loaves, John and I both said we would go, so we went along together with a clean herring basket between us. I took the opportunity to ask John how I would know if I was saved.

'Well,' he said, 'If thou shalt confess with thy mouth the Lord Jesus and shalt believe in thine heart that God hath raised Him from the dead, thou shalt be saved' (Romans 10:9).

'I really don't know what all that means, but last night I trusted the Lord Jesus as my Saviour.' John immediately dropped the basket and stretched out his hand. We shook hands very firmly and John said, 'You are a brother of mine!' I'm sure that was the happiest moment of my life; the old life was forever behind me with all its attractions.

Sometimes when we think of testimony, we reflect on what a man was, but real testimony is what a man is now by the grace of God.

Alex B. McLean

6

Which Light is Flashing for You—RED or GREEN?

W HEN YOU ARE COMING into Peterhead harbour from the north at night time there's a sectored flashing light on the North Pier. If the green light is flashing as you approach the harbour you are on the right course and you will make the harbour safely. If the red light is flashing as you approach, then you are off course and if you remain on the same course you will end up on the rocks.

Believers on the Lord Jesus, the green light is flashing for you and you are on the way to heaven, 'and they shall never perish' (John 10:28).

Sinner friend, the red light is flashing for you and if you carry on your course you will end up in hell: 'If ye repent not, ye shall all perish...' (Luke 13:5). You have to 'consider your ways' (Haggai 1:6). The red light flashing is the warning light. How many warnings have you had? You may think that you are on the right course, 'There is a way that seemeth right unto a man but the end thereof is the ways of death' (Proverbs 16:25). The devil would whisper to you and tell you not to pay attention and that in the end all will be all right. How many have perished on the rocks and are now in hell because they listened to the lies of Satan.

If a boat does not pay heed to the red flashing light it will end up on the rocks, shipwrecked. If you do not pay heed to God's warnings you will find yourself in hell—too late to be saved then, 'Between **us** and **you** there is a great gulf fixed' (Luke 16:26). The **us** refers to **believers in paradise** and the **you** refers to the **unbelievers in hades**.

It would be wise for you to 'Let thine eyes look right on' (Proverbs 4:25) and see the folly of the course that you are on.

The boat is now shipwrecked—too late now to change course, but may you come to know Jesus Christ as your Lord and Saviour before you too are shipwrecked and lost eternally. With great concern for your never dying soul may you, 'Ponder the path of thy feet' (Proverbs 4:25).

G.M.

7

The Fisherman's Hymn

D URING THE REVIVAL on the north coast of Scotland a
hymn was frequently sung called the 'Fisherman's
Hymn'. The warm-hearted converted fishermen who
brought the gospel message from port to port did not
know the author of it so they called it 'The Fisherman's
Hymn'. The last few words of each verse ended 'Jesus died
for me'.

> Once I walked in the paths of darkness,
> Sin and misery,
> Till from Calvary came the tidings
> Jesus died for me.
>
> Can it be the world's Creator
> Groaned upon the tree?
> Is it true this wondrous message
> Jesus died for me?
>
> Brethren spread the fame of Jesus,
> Wondrous Saviour He,
> Tell throughout the world these tidings
> Jesus died for me.

A simple hymn used of God at that time.

8

Peace

IN THE SUMMER of 1989 we sailed for the fishing grounds aboard the vessel 'Graceful'. At the time we were involved in pair trawling which is where the net is pulled by two boats. We were fishing for white fish.

When we left the port of Fraserburgh it was a nice summer's day which all fishermen love; but when we reached the fishing grounds, the weather changed and the wind had agitated a light swell on the sea.

We began fishing and our net became tangled during the first haul; the second haul we broke our warp. One of the crew said, 'Things always come in threes.' The other boat shot their net and so we started going towards it to pick up the other end; at this point I was going up to the top deck to throw a line overboard when the boat took a lurch and I fell overboard into the water.

When the crew saw what had happened, the alarm was raised that Johnie was in the water. The skipper quickly turned the boat around without any panic, for he knew that Johnie was no stranger to water. He came round and picked me up, but five minutes is quite a long time when you are in the water. There was a verse of Scripture came into my mind, 'Thou wilt keep in perfect peace the mind stayed on thee' (Isaiah 26:3).

When the crew pulled me back on board the fishing boat, they could not understand why I was so calm. Have you, dear reader, made peace with God? Have you known the forgiveness of sins, repentance towards God and faith in our Lord Jesus Christ?

J. Cowe
Gardenstown

9

A Voice from the Deep

T HE FISHING BOAT 'Helen Anne' left Stornoway from the herring fishing and was heading back to Findochty. The skipper, Sandy Pirie, with his two sons and four other men formed the crew. Pirie was an earnest Christian and preached God's glorious gospel.

As they left Stornoway the weather was good and the sea was calm; all on board were looking joyfully for the moment of their safe return to their homes. Entering the dangerous waters of the Pentland Firth they sailed on and into the narrow channel between the Isle of Stroma and the mainland, and found themselves suddenly enveloped in a dense fog. Owing to the thick mist and the strong current which was running some nine or ten knots an hour, it was impossible to make out their exact position.

Suddenly at about nine o'clock at night there was a tremendous crash against the outer sunken rock of the 'Men of May' at St. John's Point. Pirie hoped for a moment to be able to steer the boat into a neighbouring inlet but the keel was so injured that the water rushed into her and she began to sink. Sudden, violent death stared them in the face. The floats used with the fishing nets were hastily seized and fastened round their bodies. It was only just in time. The skipper's younger son, Jamie, a lad of eighteen years of age looked piteously into his father's face, his countenance speaking more than words. Pirie could only say, 'Jamie look to the Lord, my boy, look to the Lord.' As the boat sank, the crew, as best they could, hung on to the buoys and loose planks.

They cried for help, and Pirie with heart uplifted to God, prayed earnestly and aloud that He would send help and deliverance in their deep distress. Happy in his own spirit knowing whom he had believed, his two boys weighed heavily on his mind, although he trusted that they were under the shelter of the blood of Christ. As the tide rapidly carried Pirie away from the rest of the crew and the darkness obscured him from their view, he raised his voice in praise to God, singing that beautiful verse:

> Lord Jesus to tell of thy love
> Our souls shall for ever delight,
> And sing of thy glory above
> In praises by day and by night.
> Wherever we follow Thee Lord,
> Admiring, adoring, we see
> That love which was stronger than death
> Flow out without limit and free.

His two poor sons were filled with alarm as they lost sight of their beloved father; both were clinging to a spar, one at each end, but Jamie, the younger, who had been acting as cook on board, and was therefore the more thinly clad, soon succumbed to the exposure, and quitting his hold, he fell back exhausted into the sea and perished. One of the other four of the crew, who was a Christian, pointed the others to the Saviour and told them in his simple way of the finished work of the Lord Jesus Christ and that there was yet time to believe on Him and be saved.

Cries were heard by a gamekeeper ashore and a search was put out, and the fog having lifted they saw five poor fellows clinging on to a spar. Two of them were on the edge of exhaustion and Jamie had perished. They were safely rescued. Was there any possibility of finding Pirie, or had he succumbed and perished like Jamie? They eventually picked him up some miles from where the boat had sunk; a few more moments and it would have been too late. For two long hours Pirie had found himself carried further and further away. Eternity stared him in the face. They were testing moments but the grace of his Saviour had sustained him and the knowledge of His wondrous love kept him during that terrible ordeal. At last being nearly to the mouth in the water, with night coming on, the thought pressed upon him to quit hold of the buoys and end the struggle; but life is dear and he felt afterwards that it had been the suggestion of Satan. Lifting up his heart to God, he thought that He meant to keep him in this world. Looking round in a semi-conscious state, he saw a boat apparently about to run right over him; but all were keeping a sharp look out, and through the Lord's infinite mercy they had steered straight to him. He was taken aboard and the rescued were soon all conveyed ashore not far from John O'Groats, and restored with medical aid from the effects of the long immersion.

The news of the rescue spread far and wide and the following Sunday—it having been made known that Pirie would preach—a large crowd of people from many miles around assembled in the open air. Barely recovered from the ordeal and sore at heart at the loss of his son, he scarcely knew how to speak, but seeking grace from God, the word went forth from his lips with power.

Turning to the young people present, he said, 'Dear young people, if you were to die tonight, where would you go? Are you ready, are you prepared to meet God?' Then to the aged he said, 'You dear people who are on the threshold of eternity, are you ready? I'm not asking you what your life has been or what you've done or haven't done in life, but I do ask, Have you been cleansed by Christ's precious blood?' And to the anxious, he pointed out the way of salvation, illustrating it by his own condition in the sea when the boat came—how glad he was to let go of the feeble support he had clung to and allow strong hands to save him.

Yes dear reader, this is the simple way to be saved. Your case is hopeless: you cannot save yourself. The strong arm of the Lord alone can deliver you. Will you trust it? To remain as you are is to perish eternally, to die in your sins without hope.

The next day a boat having come to take him home, Pirie parted from his new found friends with tears. God alone knows the results of that day's meetings. And now beloved reader, we would appeal to you once again. How is it with you? Are you ready? Are you still a poor sinner ready to perish, or have you believed on the Son of God? If not, then once more you have the opportunity. Tomorrow may be too late. God's time is now.

> Time is earnest, passing by,
> Death is earnest, drawing nigh,
> Sinner wilt thou trifling be?
> Time and death appeal to thee.
> Oh, be earnest! death is near,
> Thou wilt perish, lingering here,
> Sleep no longer, rise and flee,
> Lo thy Saviour waits for thee.

G.M.

10

Distress Channel

2,182 KHz or Channel 16 VHF

'MAYDAY' IS THE DISTRESS SIGNAL. Sent three times when a ship is in danger, it requires immediate assistance.

The DISTRESS CALL comprises:

a. The distress signal 'Mayday' spoken 3 times
b. The words 'This is'
c. The name of the ship in distress spoken 3 times

I want to tell you that the distress channel to heaven is still open for the sinner who cries to be saved from his sins.

Who can use the distress channel to heaven? Is it just certain persons? **'FOR EVERYONE WHOSOEVER**, who shall call on the name of the Lord, shall be saved' (Romans 10:13). Jesus is able, willing and ready to save you; He is listening for your cry of distress: 'In my distress I called upon the Lord...he heard my voice...and my cry came before him' (Psalm 18:6). It does not matter how bad you have been: 'Not all thy sin's dark story has turned away his love.' Nor does it matter how far you have sunk in sin. **JESUS** loves the sinner and loves to answer any cry of distress and save the sinner from his sins: 'Then they cried unto the Lord in their trouble and he saved them out of their distresses' (Psalm 107:13).

The Bible has many records of people who used the distress channel to heaven. Bartimaeus in Luke 18 cried out: 'Jesus have mercy on me.' The dying thief next to Jesus on the cross in Luke 23 said, 'Remember me Lord'.

The tax-gatherer in Luke 18 prayed, 'O God have compassion on me, the sinner.' And Peter in Matthew 14 beginning to sink cried out saying, 'Lord save me.'

You too may use the distress channel while it is still the day of opportunity, and be saved for time and eternity. You will never regret it; it will be the best decision you will ever make.

This book has many testimonies of persons who used the distress channel.

DO IT NOW BEFORE IT IS TOO LATE

G.M.

11

My Experience and Conversion

'Call upon me in the day of trouble: I
will deliver thee' (Psalm 50:15).

I T IS NOT MY DESIRE to call attention to myself, but to point any who read this, who have no link with the Lord Jesus, to Him, that they may turn to this wonderful Saviour God.

I was a young lad in my 'teens; my father and mother were lovers of Jesus and their whole concern was that the family should learn to love Him, too. The prayers of my mother were going to follow me.

I was soon to leave school to go out into the world and was at a crossroads in my life. There was the signpost, one arm pointing to Jesus and heaven, the way everlasting, the other to Satan and a lost eternity. When Jesus went to heaven after He arose from the grave, God sent the Holy Spirit to convict the world of sin and of righteousness and of judgment. After going to the cinema with my companions one Saturday afternoon I came home at night and went to bed. The Holy Spirit began to work on my soul. I wet the pillow with my tears and said to myself, 'If Jesus comes tonight and if I am not saved, I will be lost for ever.' My resolve was not to go to the cinema again.

The next Saturday came and my companions called for me, and I was overcome by the enemy of our souls and I yielded and went with them. When I returned that night, again I passed through the same experience—the Spirit of God called again—but I did not yield to Him. Before

35

falling asleep that night, I felt the burden of sin lying heavily on me, and the thought was filling my mind, 'If the Lord comes tonight, and my sins are unpardoned, it will be a lost eternity for me.'

> 'Too late, too late, will be the cry,
> Jesus of Nazareth has passed by.'

But, as usual, I brushed the Holy Spirit aside. He might not have called again. 'My Spirit', says God, 'shall not always plead with man' (Genesis 6:3). So it may be if God is seeking you and you refuse His 'still, small voice', He may have to use the harder way, as He did with me.

At the age of fourteen I went to sea. Six whole years went by, unconverted years. At the age of twenty I went to the west coast aboard a steam drifter, line fishing. We left Mallaig one very stormy day to shoot our lines at the Isle of Rona, a three or four hours' sail. (I usually wore stiff leather boots which needed a help to pull off, but a voice seemed to say this day, "Put on a new rubber pair," which I had, but which I had never worn.) It was Saturday afternoon and a strong southerly gale was blowing. With much difficulty we got the lines shot into the sea and were steaming full speed broadside to the wind and waves for the anchorage. Most of the crew of eleven had gone under cover, but somehow three of us stayed a while longer on the lee-side of the wheelhouse. The other two decided to go below also and I was left alone. Just as I was going to move aft too, a 'large sea' struck the vessel, heeling her over, so that the whole lee-side went below the water, and I was carried right over the stern into the boiling sea. As I surfaced I caught sight of the boat, smoke belching from the funnel, with the sail filled with wind, steaming away full speed.

Left alone now, I was more often below the water than above, having great difficulty in getting breath and swallowing water continually. It was evident I could not stand this for long. The sea-boots weighed heavily but I managed to kick them off. After a little while, feeling very tired, I thought about going down, but decided to stick it until I was unconscious and then go down to a watery grave. A little while longer, being about 'all-in', with a small flock of seagulls above my head, I was just about giving up. My mother's prayers were about to be answered. All at once I remembered the words of an old hymn:

> 'Can it be, Oh blessed Saviour,
> One without Thee dares to die?'

I looked up into the sky, with tears flowing down my cheeks. 'Well,' I said to myself, 'I don't know You, Jesus, but I will know You now. If ever I need Thee, my Jesus, 'tis now.' So my cry was, 'Save me, Jesus, save me.' I could hardly get my breath and went well under with every wave that came. But it was just as though He took hold of my hand—He never turned a soul away. A marvellous thing happened! I do not remember going down again. All went in my favour. The boat being well away, was coming back but found no trace of me until someone pointed to the little flock of birds up into the wind. There was God's mark; He never makes mistakes. A lifebuoy was thrown and a wave came and washed me right into it, then willing hands drew me aboard, where I praised the Lord while being carried below. This was an experience that changed my life.

Oh, dear reader, what a God He is, dwelling in purest light! Far-flung heavens cannot hold Him; He upholds all things by the might of His power. This is the God who has made Himself known in the Person of His Son. The 'Lord of Glory, who could'st leave, the height supreme in death to lie.' Have you ever seen love like this? He died for my sins and yours, if you put your trust in Him. 'God is not willing that any should perish but that all men might be saved.'

I trust, dear reader, if you have no link with Christ, that by reading this you also will give Him, 'your soul, your life, your all.'

George West
Fraserburgh

12

Lighthouses

DOTTED ALONG THE COAST of the British Isles are lighthouses. They are not appreciated nowadays by fishermen as they used to be because of all the modern equipment we now carry.

The lighthouse shines out a beam across the sea warning the sailor of the rocks ahead. Heaven's lighthouse is shining a beam across the dark waters of sin to you as your tiny frail bark nears the rocks of a lost eternity, 'and light shall shine upon thy ways' (Job 22:28).

Do not be foolish and continue your course against the light. Many birds fly into the lighthouse light and are killed. What folly to run against light and pay no heed to the shining beams. Oh, the need for you to be awakened to the awful position you're in: 'Wake up...and the Christ shall shine upon you' (Ephesians 5:14).

G.M.

Psalm 23—
Fisherman's Version

THE LORD is my Pilot; I shall not drift,
   He lighteth me across the dark waters;
He steereth me in deep channels.
He keepeth my log.
He guideth me by the star of holiness
For His Name's sake.
Yea, though I sail mid the thunders and tempests of life
I will dread no danger, For Thou art with me,
Thy love and care, they shelter me.
Thou preparest a harbour before me in the homeland
Of eternity.
Thou anointest the waves with oil,
My ship rideth calmly.
Surely sunlight and starlight shall favour me on the voyage.
And I will rest in the port of my God for ever.

Captain J. Roberts

14

Setting the Course

NOWADAYS IN THE FISHING FLEET, most boats have video plotters to plot their courses when steaming and towing. It was not all that long ago that you used a chart table and chart. When you came out of the harbour, you fixed your position where you were going to start fishing, and put a line on the chart and **SET YOUR COURSE**.

On the journey of life across the sea of time, we have to set our course; to set our course we must look at our chart—at our Bible, which is God's word. On that journey there are two destinations—**HEAVEN** and **HELL**.

I ask you, which course are you on—**HEAVEN** or **HELL**?

WHITHER BOUND? There's no middle course; it has to be one or the other.

You may be unsure about which course you are on. If you have a link with the Lord Jesus as your Saviour, then you are **HEAVEN BOUND**. If you have not, then you are **HELL BOUND** and you need to alter course **NOW**. 'Behold, now is the accepted time: behold, now is the day of salvation'.

There was a man in the Bible called Pilate and he asked the question, 'What then shall I do with Jesus?' (Matthew 27:22). Your course depends on what you do with Jesus. You can either accept Him or reject Him, but remember your eternal destiny hangs upon this decision.

ETERNITY
WITHOUT CHRIST—NO HOPE

Which way are you **SETTING YOUR COURSE**?

G.M.

15

Old Sea Dog's Last Call

TAKEN ILL, and lying in mid ocean, death staring him in the face; that was the condition of John Coutts who was the wild, swearing type of sea-captain. He winced in the presence of death, and fear of 'the beyond' took hold of him. At last he sent for the first officer and said, 'Williams, get on your knees and pray a bit for a fellow. I'm awfully bad: expect I'll go this time.'

'I'm not a praying man, captain, I can't pray.'

'Well bring me a Bible and read me a bit, my hopes run out.'

'I've no Bible, captain.'

'Well then send the second officer here, perhaps he can pray a bit.'

The second officer then stood by his bunk.

'Say Thomas, I'm afraid I'm bound for eternity this trip, get down and pray if you can.'

'I'd do it captain, if I could,' said the second officer; but since he was a lad he had never prayed.

'Have you a Bible then?' said the captain.

'No sir.'

'Then tell the third officer I want to see him,' said the captain.

The third officer, like his superiors, could not pray and had no Bible. They searched the ship for a man that prayed or had a Bible.

At last one of the men came and said he had seen a book just like the Bible in the hands of the cook's boy, Willie Platt.

'Just see if he has one,' said the captain.

'Sonny, have you got a Bible?'

'Yes,' said the boy, 'but I only read it in my own time.'

'Oh that's all right boy. Fetch it and sit down here and find something that will help me; I'm going to die. Find something about God having mercy on sinners. Read it boy!'

Poor boy! He didn't know where to read, but remembering his mother had often made him read the 53rd chapter of Isaiah, Willie turned to that chapter and read. He got to the fifth verse: 'But he was wounded for our transgressions, he was bruised for our iniquities: the chastisement of our peace was upon him; and with his stripes we are healed.'

The captain who had been listening for his life, realising that he was certainly having his last chance said, 'Stop boy! Now that sounds like it. Read it again.'

Once again Willie read the words of verse five to him.

'Aye boy, that's good. That's it.'

Willie then got braver and said, 'Captain, when I was reading that verse at home, mother made me put my name in it. May I put it in now just where mother told me?'

'Certainly sonny, go on, put your name in just where she told you.'

Reverently the boy read, 'He was wounded for Willie Platt's transgressions, he was bruised for Willie Platt's iniquities; the chastisement of Willie Platt's peace was upon him, and with his stripes Willie Platt is healed.'

By then as Willie finished, the captain was half over his bedside, and eagerly said, 'Boy, read again and put my name in, put your captain's name in—John Coutts, John Coutts.'

Then the boy read, 'He was wounded for John Coutts' transgressions, he was bruised for John Coutts' iniquities: the chastisement of John Coutts' peace was upon him; and with his stripes John Coutts is healed.'

Then he lay back, having heard these glorious words ringing in his ears. He over and over repeated them putting his own name in; and as he did so, the joys of heaven

filled the heart of a new-born soul. Another sinner for
whom Christ died had now believed Him and received
Him: 'But as many as received him, to them gave he the
right to be children of God' (John 1:12).

A few days later the soul of the captain passed away
and he was buried at sea; the captain had gone to be with
Jesus. Can you put your name into Isaiah 53:5?

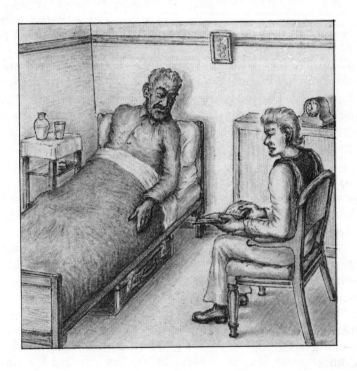

16

A Friend at All Times

WE WERE FISHING round the west coast of Scotland. We had taken a catch of herring and put them into one of the fish tanks on the port side with the result that the boat took on a list and moved the net, which left a space about 1½ feet wide and about 12 feet long. I told the skipper that night that I didn't understand why it had happened. The following day we were called to shoot the net. There was a rope laid out to be repaired which was lying inside the boat where I usually stand. The net just started to run when the rope came up with force and hit me about the waist and threw me into the net. I was in the net but the weight of my body kept me from going over the side. Some of the crew had seen what had happened and cried to the skipper. When he heard that I was in the net he put the boat on astern. The net was still running, but I was thrown into the space. When the net had stopped running I tried to get out but discovered I couldn't move as my leg was broken.

The preacher at the weekend gave out that hymn, 'I could not do without Thee O Saviour of the lost.' I proved that in no uncertain way as these crew members were willing to help but could do nothing, but I found One who I had known for many years as my Saviour and He was able to help and did—a friend at all times. Just before this happened I had been talking to the skipper about how the hymn, 'Rock of Ages' had been written when the hymn-writer was out in the open and the storm broke out and he saw the cleft in the rock and went into it and took shelter. When the skipper came to visit me at home, we marvelled at how the space had been prepared for me, and how these things happen to bring us closer to the Lord Jesus. It is a wonderful thing to know such a Saviour.

Peterhead Fisherman

17

Lifeline

I was wrecked on a rocky and desolate shore,
Sinking slowly beneath the wild sea,
When all my struggles and efforts were o'er,
Christ threw out the lifeline to me.

He threw out the life-line to me...
He threw out the life-line to me...
From Calvary's tree, far over the sea,
Christ threw out the life-line to me.

The billows were dashing, the waves rolling high,
No help from the land could I see,
When hope had all vanished and danger was nigh,
Christ threw out the lifeline to me.

When all was confusion midst dark billows' roll,
No light through the gloom could I see,
By trusting him fully he rescued my soul,
Christ threw out the lifeline to me.

Your sins like the billows around you may rise,
And dangers your frail barque pursue,
There's one who will heed you, and hear your faint cries;
He'll throw out the lifeline to you.

18

John Noble Stephen: Lost at Sea 3 July, 1956

W E LEFT PETERHEAD on the fishing boat 'Sustain'; a new, well-built boat. John Noble, as he was known, slept in the aft of the cabin and as the cabin came almost to a point at that end, my bunk and his were very close. This enabled us to converse quite easily. I had been saved for two years and John, by then, being well acquainted with the Word of God, was a great help to me.

We were steering in a north-easterly direction. It was a lovely night with no wind but just a slight swell—an ordinary night for us. After supper, John and I went up on deck for fresh air; most of the herring fleet were coming astern of us. I asked John a very unusual question: 'I wonder what would happen if someone was to fall overboard?'

His reply was, 'Some of the boats coming astern would pick you up.'

I said, 'Oh John, they would never see you—a head bobbing up and down. I wonder what would be the first thing you would do?'

John said, 'The first thing you would do is pray.'

I agreed and replied, 'I suppose your prayer would be like that of Stephen in Acts 7:59: "Lord Jesus, receive my spirit." '

John gave a little smile and said, 'That's right.'

It was almost time to shoot the nets; it was our job and we loved it. I said, 'What is on your mind?'; knowing that he would quote something from the Word of God.

He said, 'This is what's on my mind: "Let not the wise

man glory in his wisdom, neither let the mighty man glory in his might, let not the rich man glory in his riches: But let him that glorieth glory in this, that he understandeth and knoweth me, that I am the Lord" ' (Jeremiah 9:23).

We then shot the ninety drift nets overboard in order to catch herring. He and I rushed aft to hoist the mizen sail in order to keep the ship's head through the wind. John had previously insisted that the loosening of the sail would be his job because of the possible danger, so he jumped up on the ship's small boat and smartly unfurled the sail, but on descending his foot slipped and he fell overboard. By this time, the rope on the bow attached to the nets came tight and the boat was swinging away from John. He was not a swimmer, although he made an attempt; none of the rest of us could swim either, but John's brother Campbell quickly grabbed a life belt and jumped overboard but, alas he was too late.

John Noble was called home to be with the Lord whom he loved and served. Such was the life-work of a young man of twenty-five who made every moment count in the Lord's service and testified continually to the saving power of the Lord Jesus.

'Remember your leaders who have spoken to you the word of God; and considering the issue of their conversation, imitate their faith' (Hebrews 13:7).

Some time later, his dear mother, Mrs Stephen, went upstairs to John's room to look over his things. There was his diary just as he had left it before sailing that day. The words found in the last page were two verses from different hymns:

No future but glory Lord Jesus have we,
How bright is the prospect of being with Thee,
Oh home of all homes with the Father above,
What wonderful dwelling of infinite love.

Past death, past sin with all its woes,
O'erthrown forever all our foes,
Hope lifts our hearts to that blest day,
And takes from death its sting away.

Alex B. McLean

19

Shipping Forecasts

A T SEA WE RECEIVE four shipping forecasts a day on Radio 4, and sometimes special gale warnings at different times of the day. In the winter we get three-day forecasts from Stonehaven Radio every night or morning.

A few years ago we were fishing north of the Forties oil rigs about ninety miles ENE from Peterhead for prawns and fish. It was October and fishing was good, with a large fleet of boats at work.

Up to Wednesday night it had been a lovely week of weather but that night the forecast was for storm-force winds on Thursday night. With the sea so calm and the fishing good, we decided along with a lot of other boats to carry on fishing. Some of the fishing boats that never normally came out that distance went away in. We fished until six o'clock on Thursday evening when we heard the shipping forecast for the Forties—severe gale 9 to violent storm 11: a very, very bad forecast.

We arrived into Fraserburgh on Friday morning after a good pounding. The wind was so strong that the boxes on the pier were going everywhere. There were some record wind speeds recorded in different parts. We heard in the harbour that one of the boats we were fishing along with and were only a couple of miles from when we began steaming in, was missing with all aboard feared drowned. After an air and sea search failed to find anything, it was called off. Another tragedy with parents losing sons, wives losing husbands and children losing fathers—**YET WARNED**.

God is giving many warnings to sinners. We are using this book to warn you of a coming judgment: 'Blow the trumpet and warn the people' (Ezekiel 33:3). How can we escape from the judgment to come? 'Jesus, our deliverer from the coming wrath' (1 Thessalonians 1:10).

God used Noah to warn the people of judgment to come and yet only eight souls were saved. God used Jonah to warn Ninevah of judgment: 'Yet forty days, and Ninevah shall be overthrown' (Jonah 3:4).

But, alas, many are not paying attention to the warnings. 'He heard the sound of the trumpet and took not warning' (Ezekiel 33:5). What happens to those who don't pay attention to God's warnings? 'But if thou warn the wicked of his way to turn from it, and he does not turn from his way, he shall die in his iniquity' (Ezekiel 33:9).

If you die in your sins you will be raised in your sins and heaven's door will be shut to you forever, because only those whose sins are washed away by Jesus' blood will be there.

Do not go on rejecting the pleas of a Saviour God who loves you and wants to save you: 'Our Saviour God, who desires that all men should be saved' (1 Timothy 2:4).

The captain of the 'Lusitania' is a fitting story of one who rejected a warning. He received a message while in New York that his great ship would be torpedoed before he reached Britain—he laughed at the idea—but it was true—**DO NOT REJECT THE WARNINGS FROM GOD.**

G.M.

20

On Course to Jesus

'THAT IS THE END of the Shipping Forecast'. Words that down through the years I have heard many times. A VHF radio crackles into life. 'That's a poor forecast lads,' is the opinion held by most of us. Then another voice speaks, 'Never mind lads—it's just a prediction not a promise.' Yes, being a fisherman has its benefits, but alas it has its drawbacks; the shipping forecast being only one of many. That was how it was with me, before I accepted Christ as my Saviour. Let me tell you of my meeting with the Saviour; twice in fact and both times on my knees in a toilet!

As a skipper of a fishing boat in 1979 I used to be very easy going, or so I thought. I gambled a little, played quite a lot of golf, much of it at the 19th hole, took a drink— sometimes too much. In the eyes of the world I was really quite sociable. What I also did was to take home with me the pressures of the fishing, the poor forecasts, net problems, next week's fishing plan and many more work associated problems.

To relieve these pressures I went for a drink and it was on the 20th January 1979 that the Lord first spoke to me in the local hotel.

Earlier that day I had had some very disturbing news, a friend of mine, a fellow skipper and a pal since our childhood days, arrived home from hospital where he had undergone tests for a sore back. As it turned out he was terminally ill. I could not understand it; all I wanted to do was blot it out of my mind; so I went out for a 'pint' with that intention: maybe things would change after a few drinks.

Change they did! In a most unexpected way. I was standing at the bar when suddenly I felt violently sick. I rushed through to the toilet and locked the door. The sickness was so intense that I was forced to my knees; suddenly that small confined space was filled with a brilliant shining light and out of its midst a voice spoke to me asking, 'Ian, why are you vomiting down a toilet? This won't change anything, you could spend your life in a far better way.' I was speechless, but I knew that I was in a presence far greater than I had ever been before. 'This must be God speaking', I thought, 'so I must do something to change my life.'

On my knees, in the toilet of a local hotel, I made my decision for Christ.

I left that hotel trembling, knowing I couldn't just go home, or by the morning I would have put it down to too much drink; so I phoned a fellow skipper—a Christian; three times I tried to get him but without success. He later told me that he had gone with some friends for a meal, but would have been more than glad to have travelled the thirty miles to help me.

As I left the phone box a voice kept saying, 'Forget it, Ian, no one wants to hear your story. Go back and have a few more drinks.' That was Satan trying his hardest to win me back. 'No'—I must tell someone. I needed help from a Christian so I phoned another man, this time a neighbour, and his son informed me that his parents were out. Satan must have been overjoyed at this. I started to make my way home and all the way the Holy Spirit kept at me, 'Don't give up, Ian, tell someone'; so I walked past my own door where my wife and at that time two children were, my wife worried sick as to what state I would arrive home; sometimes I was very aggressive when drunk.

I arrived at the neighbour's house. Again the door was opened by their son who invited me in and phoned his parents. That boy was used by the Lord that night. After about ten to fifteen minutes the couple arrived home and the wife made me a strong cup of coffee while her husband told me that it was the Lord that had spoken to me earlier in that toilet. He told me what I now needed to do in my life.

We later both went round to my home and told my wife of what had happened. Later she told me that she had been praying for some time that a change would occur in my life. Kneeling down later that night when we were alone, I prayed for the first time in my life to ask God's forgiveness for all the heartache and trouble I had caused. Next morning I went to church with my wife. I don't remember what the sermon text was but I do remember thinking that every word the minister spoke was totally about me: a sinner saved by grace.

When the service was over, I left the church drenched in sweat, feeling very guilty and, plucking up the courage, I went to see my friend who was terminally ill. 'Come awa in and give us all yer news' was how he greeted me. I told him of my conversion the previous evening. His answer to this left me feeling very humble. He spoke words that I will never forget. 'Ian,' he said, 'That is the best news I ever heard.' Those were some of the last words he spoke to me. A short time later he went to be with the Lord, having accepted Christ himself during his illness.

For many months I was overjoyed at walking with the Lord, but I was to make a serious mistake, allowing Satan a foothold in my life again. It all came about because of a friend's remark after a gospel service and my wrong interpretation; I then reckoned that I could live my life 50/50, half for the Lord and the other half to enjoy the pleasures of the world. I was to become a backslider for a time until once again God was to intervene. One night during this time I had been socialising and went to phone my wife to come and take me home; I dialled the number which I thought was my own and I heard a voice at the other end say, 'Is that you Ian Mair? Where are you tonight?' I recognised the voice of a friend who since that time, along with his wife, have been like a father and mother to me during my walk with the Lord. 'Don't you move until I come and get you,' he said but I did and I don't know why—God's will I suspect; and I arrived at his door. His wife made me most welcome, but when he arrived back he proceeded to give me a good telling-off, something which I resented. He later took me home and duly gave me another dressing down in front of my wife. This made me really angry and I can remember threatening to throw him out if he didn't leave. Satan must have been ecstatic at all this aggression.

When he left I felt very sick and ran to the toilet in my own home. There on my knees, the Lord spoke to me once again and out of the same brilliant shining light asked me the question, 'My way or your way, Ian?' Trembling I answered, 'Your way, Lord.'

Having seen the 'light' twice it has been my great privilege and joy to serve the Lord with all my heart and soul. The Lord must have had a reason to appear and intervene in my life twice. One day I will stand before Him in Glory and praise Him for the saving grace so amply bestowed on this sinner.

To end I need to rearrange some words I started with: The Lord's forecast is a PROMISE and not a Prediction.

Ian Mair

21

Hymn

Fierce and wild the storm is raging round the
 helpless bark,
On to doom is swiftly driving o'er the waters dark,
Joy O Joy Behold the Saviour,
Joy O Joy the message hear,
I'll stand by until the morning I've come to save
 you—do not fear.

T HAT HYMN was written partly due to the following
story:

All at once those on the wreck were cheered and comforted for from another vessel there came across the wave
the welcome cry 'I've come to save you, I'll stand by you
until the morning.'

How thankful we are that the Lord Jesus stood by us
when we cried out in distress of soul to be saved. The
Lord Jesus didn't wait until the morning; He saved us
immediately.

22

Whither Bound?

A VERY IMPORTANT QUESTION to the present age. Life is not static, often unstable and likened to a voyage. Autumn leaves fly before the gale; snowflakes are driven in the storm; waves are spent on the shore. Only man has the responsibility to give an answer, not through chance but by choice.

The latter part of the twentieth century has seen the world caught in a maddening momentum with circumstances virtually out of control, but alas—Whither Bound?

The following story tells of a tragic voyage from which some spiritual lessons may be observed.

The loss of the Aberdeen trawler 'Ben Doran' with all hands, foundering on the dreaded Vee Skerries, Shetland, 29th March 1930.

The Loss of The Ben Doran

Many songs have been written and tales have been told
Of shipwrecks, disasters and heroes so bold,
And oft times our eyes have been melted to tears
By stories of suffering, of dangers and fears.
But ne'er has been told a more pitiful tale,
Of a vessel that sank in the teeth of a gale,
Than the trawler, Ben Doran, a smart fishing smack
That went down off the Skerries with all hands on deck.

Many similar trips the Ben Doran had made,
As this fatal trip, as she followed her trade,
And oft times before stormy billows had raged,
But what mattered the tempest to men thus engaged?

For children and wives must be sheltered and fed
And fish must be caught if they'd earn them their bread
So the Ben Doran's crew often sailed the North Sea
Not stopping to think what the weather might be.

Jim Caie was the skipper, a God-fearing man
And one who in his youth had accepted God's plan
Of salvation through faith in the blood of His Son,
And not through self-merits or works he had done.
Kind husband, good father, a brave man at sea,
Skilled master and skipper all knew him to be.
He knew the rough seas and where rocks would be found
As he sailed past the Orkneys to good fishing ground.

Outside of the skipper, the Ben Doran's crew
Was composed of eight men, brave, loyal, and true
With weather-tanned faces, courageous and bold
But whose each manly frame, a kind heart did hold,
Most all had some children, all but one had loved wives,
For whose sake these men oft endangered their lives
As they left their loved lassies and bairnies so wee
As with the Ben Doran they put out to sea.

On that ill-fated trip when she perished at sea,
The Ben Doran as usual had sailed down the Dee
Past Footdee, past Torry, then crossing the bar,
Then into the rough sea for Shetland so far;
And some as they kissed their loved ones so dear
Had said they'd a strange foreboding of fear,
But none could foretell what her fate was to be
As she sailed from the Fishmarket out to the sea.

The skipper had made it a practice for years
At the end of each week, to allay his wife's fears
To telegraph home and to say all was well,
And, oh, how their hearts were now stricken with fear
As Saturday passed and no word reached their ear—

Anxiety, anguish, suspense hard to bear,
As they thought of the dark night and their loved ones
—Where?

The first that was known of the Ben Doran's plight
As the seas dashed upon her with fury and might
Was when on the Skerries her form was descried
As the waves beat upon her and over her side,
T'was the Brackenbush crew who first saw her wreck
And they said that the wave was awash o'er her deck,
For the sea raged in fury in masses of white,
And their hearts were dismayed at that terrible sight.

Unable to reach them, this boat hurried back,
Across the St. Magnus for aid of the wreck;
For forms could be seen hanging on to the mast
Midst tempest and spray, and snow, sleet and blast.
The Aurora set out across the rough bay,
As also a motor boat under Theodore Kay,
But try as they might, to get to her side
Was a task beyond men, in that tempest and tide.

As night followed day, they still clung to the wreck
Holding on to the rigging as waves swept the deck,
The day followed darkness and still they were there
The subject of Shetland's intercession and prayer.
A life boat sets out and a sea-going plane
But, alas, every effort at rescue is vain,
For feeble and weak, they relinquished their hold
And sink at the last in the waters so cold.

What thoughts must have filled each dear fellow's mind
As he saw in the distance the seamen so kind,
So willing to help but so powerless to aid
And as hope of their rescue begins now to fade.
They think of their homes, as they cling for their lives,
Of their wee lads and lassies, their mothers and wives,

Of the friends and the faces they'll see never more,
For now they are entering Eternity's shore.

Do thoughts of Eternity rush through the mind
And thoughts of a God who is holy and kind?
Do they think of His goodness in giving His Son
To save them from hell, lost sinners, undone?
How earnest our wish that every brave man
On that ill-fated vessel accepted the Lamb
God's blest Lamb of God, who on Calvary's tree
Procured their redemption that we might be free.

Their friends were so willing, those dear men to save
And to rescue their lives from a watery grave,
Heroic the efforts, but lacking the power
To save them from death in danger's fraught hour.
But Jesus the Saviour, God's only blest Son
Completed salvation, left nothing undone
To save us from death, He sank 'neath death's wave
And now He is willing and able to save.

Alex Stewart

23

The Seaman's Prayer

O LORD JESUS, Thou who didst walk upon the storm-tossed ocean, come to my troubled life and bring me Thy peace.

Thou who didst call the fishermen from their nets long ago to follow Thee, help me to answer Thy call to-day.

Thou who didst enter into the boat by the seaside to preach, come, enter my heart and speak Thy word of forgiveness.

Be Thou the Captain of my soul, as I seek now to renounce sin and all its follies, henceforth to live for Thee.

I trust Thee now, by faith as my own personal Saviour. Come on board, Lord Jesus! Pilot me safely over the sea of life to the Heavenly Shore, where I shall be with Thee for ever. In Thy Name. Amen.

Noel Grant
Bangor, N.I.

24

Heaven's Lifeboat

WITH THE HELICOPTER now doing most rescues at sea, the lifeboat isn't used as much as in days gone by when many fishermen owed their lives to the lifeboat. When receiving word that a boat is in distress, they launch out into the stormy seas to try and save lives. The coxswain of a lifeboat has a very responsible and difficult job if weather conditions are poor.

Who is the coxswain of heaven's lifeboat? It is the Lord Jesus, 'Christ Jesus came into the world to save sinners' (1 Timothy 1:15). It was said of the Lord Jesus, 'who did no sin, neither was guile found in his mouth' (1 Peter 2:22). He could have gone back to heaven without dying but in love for sinners He died on the cross, shed His blood and rose as a victorious Saviour, and He is the only one who can take the helm of heaven's lifeboat, and its great mission is 'to seek and to save that which is lost' (Luke 19:10).

The lifeboat only goes out when a call of distress is put out, but heaven's lifeboat is always out searching the wild seas of time for lost, perishing souls. Heaven's lifeboat is out searching for you just now, as in the parable, the shepherd goes 'after that which is lost, until he finds it' (Luke 15:4). The coxswain—our Lord Jesus—can only save you if you give up trying to save yourself and cry to be saved; then Jesus will stop the 'boat' and take hold of you: 'And immediately Jesus stretched out his hand and caught hold of him' (Matthew 14:31). Once He takes hold of you He will never let you go. He will not look up your past life's record to see if you are worth saving, but will save you 'immediately': '…also he is able to save them to the uttermost' (Hebrews 7:25) which cry to Him.

O soul, sinking down 'neath sin's merciless wave,
The strong arm of our coxswain is mighty to save,
Then trust Him today, no longer delay,
Board the old ship of Zion, and shout on your way,

'Jesus saves!
Jesus saves!'
Shout and say on your way,
'Jesus saves!'.

When in days gone by a boat put out a distress signal a good distance from land, it took the lifeboat a good while to reach it, and even now it might take a rescue helicopter half an hour to reach a vessel in distress, but with heaven's lifeboat on the sea of time, there are no waits, it is 'immediately'.

You may have fears that once aboard you might be thrown back overboard again because you are such a sinner, but the coxswain gives you assurance, 'and him that comes to me I will not at all cast out' (John 6:37).

When the Titanic was sinking there were not enough lifeboats for everybody; the women and children were put in first. Think of the awful extremity of those still on the Titanic as she was sinking into the cold icy waters, when they were told there was not room in the lifeboats. In heaven's lifeboat there is room for all and Jesus calls out, 'Yet there is room' (Luke 14:22).

This is not always going to be the case, however, because once the Lord Jesus comes back again, heaven's lifeboat will no longer go out to save souls. Some souls that Jesus saves will be the last. Are you going to be left behind?

Imagine sinner friend, sinking into a Christless eternity with no one to save you. You had opportunities to be rescued by heaven's lifeboat and refused and now it is no longer searching the wild ocean for you. 'They cried, but there was none to save them: even unto the Lord, but he answered them not' (Psalm 18:41). Think of these words coming to you as you sink helplessly into eternity, 'none to save'; 'none to save'.

I close this article with a final appeal from the coxswain of heaven's lifeboat, our Lord Jesus Christ, 'Come to me, all ye who labour and are burdened and I will give you rest' (Matthew 11:28).

G.M.

25

Calvary

W E FISHERMEN face many dangers from the sea: stormy weather, with gales and rough seas. I often think of the words of Psalm 42:7, 'All thy waves and billows have gone over me.' The waves are the waves of the judgment of God when God dealt with sin at Calvary's cross. No one had ever passed through such a storm. Think of the words of the Lord Jesus on the cross 'My God, My God, why hast Thou forsaken me?' Forsaken for sinners like you and me. So when you look at the stormy sea, you can think of the Saviour's great love for you.

G.M.

26

The Fisher Lad's Last Song

A COMPANY OF YOUNG LADS gathered together one Sunday evening in one of their homes. Some time was spent in singing well-known hymns, each lad requesting in turn his favourite. The young lad in this true incident, requested and helped to sing lustily:

> 'Jesus Saviour pilot me
> Over life's tempestuous sea,
> Unknown waves before me roll,
> Hiding rock and treacherous shoal,
> Chart and compass come from Thee,
> Jesus Saviour pilot me!'

Little did that happy company think that they were singing these lovely lines with this young lad for the last time; for but a few hours later in the early hours of Monday morning, he with nine others of the crew of a modern and powerful fishing boat, set off on a voyage which normally would have lasted a few days but from which they never returned.

One of the fiercest storms for many years struck the fleet, and the vessel foundered with the loss of all hands, causing a tragedy which cast a heavy gloom over the locality, and affected every man and woman whose calling linked them with the sea.

Yet such happenings, tragic as they are, are undoubtedly used of God to speak to men. Will you, my reader, allow this voice to touch your heart and conscience?

We are all on a voyage—the voyage of life. How near its

close we may be no one can say, but preparation for it can be made. The young lad in the incident trusted Christ as his Saviour, and could sing from his heart:

'When at last I near the shore
And the fearful breakers roar
'Twixt me and the peaceful rest—
Then while leaning on Thy Breast,
May I hear Thee say to me—
"Fear not! I will pilot thee!" '

Dear reader, fellow traveller to eternity, were you called to face 'journey's end' suddenly and unexpectedly, would your personal **acceptance** of Christ as Saviour cause His familiar voice to sound in your ears—'Fear not, I will pilot thee'? Or would your **rejection** of Christ cause you to face the chill waters of death, alone? Alone, with no voice to reassure, no hand to bear you across? Alone to face a Christless eternity with its hopelessness and despair?

R.W.C.

27

'His Way is in the Sea'

T HE SETTING FOR THIS INCIDENT took place aboard a fishing boat off the Butt of Lewis, in which a young man named David found the Saviour. We were fishing one Monday in 1961 in the west coast waters. It had been a beautiful day. The custom when fishing seine-net was to lie at anchor at night so, along with the rest of the fishing boats, we steamed into a bay and anchored for the night. The watches were set and as daybreak approached the wind shifted to the north-west and a swell got up; David was on watch and, seeing the situation, he called the skipper. Everything happened so quickly: the engine was started and one of the deckhands slipped the anchor chain and then the engine was put on full speed astern as we were in a dangerous position. The skipper, being a Christian, looked to God for help. We were hit by three seas— one after the other—and we had hardly time to get dressed when the cabin filled with water.

I ran up on deck and decided to get out of the galley, but on looking up I saw this monster of a sea towering above the boat; I ran back inside the galley and grabbed the nearest post, thinking this was the end. I thought the water would never stop coming in, and then we were suddenly in safe waters. If ever I had a sense of angelic care it was at that time, 'Hitherto shalt thou come but no further, and here shall thy proud waves be stayed' (Job 38:11).

David had gone out ahead of us, at what time I am not sure. No doubt he had seen this sea coming as well and held on in an exposed place at the side of the wheelhouse, but he had been swept by the sea right into the stern of the boat, over the top of the winch and the rollers which lie on the boat's deck. The skipper shouted and told us that someone was injured in the stern; we ran to see and found David badly injured, lying soaked and bleeding amongst the ropes and pond boards, the deck of the boat being in a shambles.

We carried him aft to the galley and laid him down. He had been brought up in a Christian household but had never made a confession that Jesus was his Saviour. We were all young men in our late teens and early twenties, full of zeal for Christ. One of us knelt down and spoke to David to comfort him and whispered, 'If that sea had carried you overboard we would never have known if you were saved.' He looked up and said, 'Before that sea struck me I accepted Jesus as my Saviour', then he fell back too weak to say anything else.

Meanwhile the skipper had managed to alert the other fishing boats and one came alongside and we managed to transfer David. There were no rescue helicopters at that time, so one of the crew went along with him for company. It was quite a distance to go to Stornoway where he was successfully treated.

Our boat was waterlogged. The rudder was damaged, propeller shaft lost, engine stopped and the life raft lying alongside, having been swept off the deck by the heavy seas. It was only in God's mercy that we had not foundered, but a trophy of grace had been won and secured for eternity.

We were eventually towed up to Stornoway where we were put up by some kind Christian friends until the boat was temporarily repaired before sailing home.

The Psalmist says, 'His way is in the sea'. In this incident we see the power of the sea and also the power of redeeming love.

William G. Mair

28

The Message

Just visit Lossie Harbour
At the weekend when you're free,
Fishing boats you will discover
With a message, wait and see—

DAYSPRING—from the gospel writer
Would remind us of God's Son,
Bringing in a day of gladness
By salvation He has won.

TRUST—a message so important,
If in Heaven we hope to be
We must really trust the Saviour
He who died on Calvary's tree.

THRIVE—is life which keeps on growing
Every Christian should display,
As they pray and read their Bible
Growing stronger day by day.

VIGILANT—a word of warning—
Many foes would keep us back,
Seek the Saviour now for blessing
Safe in Him from all attack.

ENTERPRISING—there's no limit
To the power that Jesus gives,
With a glad heart we can serve Him
Show to all that Jesus lives.

FAME—points us forward to the day
When home with Christ above,
My voice shall tell with thousands more
The greatness of His love.

DIADEM—that crown of splendour
Shall adorn the Saviour's brow,
Every knee shall bow before Him—
Why not gladly do it now?

Jim Gault

29

The Fisherman's Perfect Cure

I N A SMALL FISHING VILLAGE on the coast of Scotland, a servant of the Lord had been making known the glad tidings of a full and free salvation through faith in the finished work of Christ. Amongst those who attended the meetings was a young fisherman named James, who got so thoroughly awakened as to his awful position that he could not find rest, night or day, 'for fear of Hell'. Wherever he went the awful fear that he might be like the rich man who, 'died and was buried. And in hell lifting up his eyes, being in torments' (Luke 16:22,23), haunted him. Setting out for sea, returning with his catch, mending his nets, eating, sleeping, waking, working; one thought and one thought only was uppermost in his mind—he was in danger of being lost eternally.

He mixed with his comrades to try and drown his conviction, but still the reality of an eternal hell seemed to haunt him continually. Being the leading spirit in a dance club, he went to the room to seek ease for his troubled mind in a dance; but dance he could not as he said, 'for fear of hell'.

Not being able to sleep or take sufficient food, his mother, little dreaming that the trouble was about his soul, and not his body; sent for the doctor, who after sounding him and finding no disease, prescribed two bottles of medicine as a cure. The medicine, of course, made no difference.

The night following the medical treatment he was again

at the gospel meeting. That night he accepted the Lord Jesus as his Saviour:

'How lost was my condition, until Jesus made me whole
There is but one physician can cure a sin-sick soul.'

When he got out, as he afterwards said, 'I thanked the Lord with all my heart I was saved', and turning to an unsaved companion he said, 'John I'm saved'. In prayer shortly after he said, 'Father, I give Thee much thanks for saving me.'

Can you thank God for saving you? If not, like James you must be terribly afraid of the awfulness of an eternity in the darkness of hell. In such a dangerous job as fishing, how can you remain unsaved?

ACCEPT THE LORD JESUS AS YOUR SAVIOUR **NOW**

30

Danger

AT NIGHT-TIME in the North Sea when you are in the area of the oil rigs you would think you are next to a large town with the lights and the large flames coming from them as they burn off the gas. But amidst all the lights and the large flames glowing in the night-time sky, there can be seen at every corner of the oil rig a distinct white flashing light which flashes out two short flashes and one long flash. It is the letter U in morse which means YOU ARE RUNNING INTO DANGER. The flashing is warning you of danger.

Sinner, the lights are flashing out to you—that YOU ARE RUNNING INTO DANGER; you are heading for an eternity in hell. What an awful prospect! Pay heed to the flashing lights and alter course by accepting the Lord Jesus as your Saviour.

You may be young, healthy, successful and ambitious and you may pay no heed to them but I exhort you to do so. You are in great danger and God may be using this book to speak to you of your eternal destiny, 'FOR GOD SPEAKETH ONCE, AND TWICE—AND MAN PERCEIVETH IT NOT—' (Job 33:14).

This may be your last opportunity of being saved and with the brevity of life and the dangers at sea, your life may be cut off and summed up like the man's in Luke. 'And the rich man died and was buried and in hades lifted up his eyes being in torments' (Luke 16:23). That is what you face if you remain in your sins, 'died...buried...hell...torments'.

O sinner, with a heartfelt appeal, consider your position as, 'RUNNING INTO DANGER' and accept Jesus into your life before it is **TOO LATE**.

G.M.

31

Personal Testimony

A UGUST 26, 1960 IS a day I shall never forget! As a direct result of the following experience, I became a changed man.

I was a fisherman, nineteen years old, sailing out of Lossiemouth on my father's boat Devotion INS 223. Since my childhood all I had wanted to be in life was a fisherman, like my father and grandfather.

On this particular day, we were fishing seventy miles north-east of Fraserburgh but due to bad weather conditions, fishing had to be abandoned and we had to make our way back to Fraserburgh. Unfortunately we never reached the port. Around midnight I was suddenly awakened by a loud crushing noise; on rushing to the deck I saw that we were on the rocks and we were being battered by waves caused by a north-easterly gale. It was immediately apparent that we were in a desperate situation. Within a matter of minutes our fishing boat was being smashed to pieces.

Seven men were on board the Devotion that night and in seconds all were facing eternity, and I knew I was facing eternity without Christ. That night I cried to the Lord for help, 'This poor man cried, and the Lord heard him, and saved him out of all his troubles' (Psalm 34:6).

This poor man cried that night: I asked the Lord to save my life and I promised God that if my life was spared I would serve Him as long as I lived.

I was washed up on the rocks at the foot of the cliffs just east of Pennan, along with two of my shipmates. It was soon evident that four of our shipmates had perished that night; my father, my uncle George, Charles, whose wife was expecting their first child, and Harry who had been married for just twenty days. The three of us huddled together to keep warm for we had little clothing on and no shoes. We were soaking wet and frightened to move because we had no idea where we were, and in the pitch darkness we were all confused; during those hours of darkness, my life, which up to that point I had taken for granted, seemed more precious.

In the early hours of the morning we made our way to the village of Pennan where we were given care and attention. The next six weeks were turmoil; two bodies had been recovered the first day, and six weeks later the other two were picked up, the last being my father. The following week we returned to sea, this time on my uncle's boat. Towards the end of that year, 4th December to be precise, I decided to go along to the church and say 'thanks' to God for saving my life, and as far as I was concerned that was going to be the end of it. I was going to make a fresh start. As I sat in the Baptist church in Lossiemouth that night I was soon under conviction of sin, keenly aware that Jesus Christ had died for the whole world, and that He died for me. I spoke to the Pastor after the service and said that I would like to come back and speak to him sometime later that week. I am eternally grateful that that man did not try and force me to make a decision there and then. He knew that the Holy Spirit was working in my life and that at God's time I would be saved from my sin.

I was going through the square in Lossiemouth with my friend and later colleague, Bill Simmonds, and we were speaking of the events of that night. I remember saying to him, 'If I go off to sea tonight, and if I lose my life, where would I spent eternity?' I knew that God had saved my life on 26 August but standing in the square that night I also knew that my soul, which is far more precious, was still in its sinful condition. I went back to the Pastor's home, knocked on the door and that night, after clearly hearing the gospel being explained to me, I knelt before

God, confessed my sin, received Jesus Christ as my Saviour and that night I passed from death unto life. I was born again. I was a new creation in Christ. A few weeks later I confessed my faith in Christ by being baptised, declaring my allegiance to my Saviour publicly. Being a Christian on board a small fishing boat I was soon put to the test; I failed many times, but through it all God has kept me and He will keep me until that day when we meet Him face to face.

During the next seven years, I pursued my career as a fisherman, met and married my wife whom I met in Church, and my life was going according to my plans. In June of that year whilst fishing off the west coast of Scotland my cousin was washed overboard and drowned. This was an event that was to shape my future. After much thought and prayer, I decided to come ashore and apply to the Royal National Mission to Deep Sea Fishermen for Christian service within the fishing industry.

For the past twenty-five years my wife and I have served the Lord through the offices of the Mission and we have had the privilege of serving fishermen and their families. We have experienced the blessing of God upon our lives, in our home and in our work.

Speaking from my own personal experience, receiving Jesus Christ as my personal Saviour was the greatest thing that has ever happened to me. Having been a Christian for over thirty years I can honestly testify that having the fellowship of the living God with me day by day through Jesus Christ, is the greatest experience that anyone can have. To have Christ in one's life is to have everything.

I trust and pray that if you have never received Christ as your Saviour, that you will think of these things.

Jim Ralph
R.N.M.D.S.F.
Aberdeen

32

A Tale of the Sea

THE SACRED DAY was ending in a village by the sea:
  The uttered benediction touched the people tenderly,
And they rose to face the sunset in the golden glowing
  west,
And then hastened to their dwellings for God's blessed
  boon of rest.

But they looked across the water, and a storm was raging
  there;
A fierce spirit moved above them—the wild spirit of the
  air;
And it lashed and shook and tore them, till they
  thundered, groaned and boomed,
And alas for any vessel in their yawning gulfs entombed!

Sad and anxious were the people, on that rocky coast of
  Wales,
Lest the dawns of coming morrows should be telling
  fearful tales,
When the sea had spent its passion, and should cast
  upon the shore
Tangled wreck and swollen victims, as it had done
  heretofore.

With the rough winds blowing round her, a brave
  woman strained her eyes,
And she saw upon the billows a large vessel fall and rise.
Oh, it did not need a prophet to tell what the end must be,
For no ship could ride in safety near that shore on such a
  sea.

Then the pitying people hurried from their homes and
    thronged the beach,
Oh, for power to cross the waters and the perishing to
    reach!
Helpless hands were wrung for sorrow; tender hearts
    grew cold with dread,
And the ship, urged by the tempest, to the fatal rock-
    shore sped.

'She has parted in the middle! Oh, the half of her goes
    down!
God have mercy! is His heaven far to seek for those who
    drown?'
Lo! when next the white, shocked faces looked with
    terror on the sea,
Only one last clinging figure on a spar was seen to be.

Nearer the trembling watchers came the wreck, across
the wave,
And the man still clung and floated, though no power on
earth could save.
'Could we send him a short message? Here's a trumpet.
Shout away.'
'Twas the preacher's hand that took it, and he wondered
what to say.

Any memory of his sermon? Firstly? Secondly? Ah, no!
There was but one thing to utter in the awful hour of
woe;
So he shouted through the trumpet, 'Look to Jesus. Can
you hear?'
And 'Ay, ay, sir!' rang the answer o'er the waters, loud
and clear.

Then they listened: 'He is singing, "Jesus, Lover of my
soul" ';
And the winds brought back the echo, 'while the nearer
waters roll',
Strange, indeed, it was to hear him, 'Till the storm of life
is past',
Singing bravely from the waters, 'Oh, receive my soul at
last!'

He could have no other refuge. 'Hangs my helpless soul
on Thee;
Leave, ah, leave me not',—the singer dropped at last into
the sea,
And the watchers, looking homeward through their eyes
by tears made dim,
Said, 'He passed to be with Jesus in the singing of that
hymn.'

33

I Won't Have to Cross Jordan Alone

Robert Strachan aged 29, April 1970

ROBERT WAS A VERY CHEERY YOUNG MAN, married, with one young son of three years old. One day when cleaning out the fish hold after landing, I asked Robert if he was saved. 'Oh aye' he said, 'I made sure of that at the Billy Graham campaign.' I assured him that was the best thing he had ever done. One night while seine net fishing, we were about to have our usual Bible reading in the cabin. The skipper, also a young man, said he would have a look on the bridge (wheelhouse) to see everything was all right. While waiting his return we sang a few hymns. Robbie started singing:

> I won't have to cross Jordan alone,
> Jesus died for my sin to atone,
> When the darkness I see,
> He'll be waiting for me,
> I won't have to cross Jordan alone.

I said to Robbie, 'You're a good singer Robbie. I've never heard that one before, sing it again!' So he sang it again. We had our reading, then went to bed, leaving a man on watch. The next morning was a really poor day: we shot and got about twelve to fifteen boxes of codling. While gutting the fish the ship took a freak wave aboard and washed three men overboard. Two were quickly rescued, but alas Robbie Strachan could not be rescued. Lost at sea. His good Christian wife Maureen took the news with Christian dignity. Robbie had been called home to be with Christ which is far better. And he did not cross Jordan alone.

Alex McLean
(Pathway)

34

Jesus Called and
I was Ready

I N A CEMETERY in the Orkney Isles, on the stone marking the grave of a young lad are the words:

JESUS CALLED AND I WAS READY

He was the youngest member of the crew of a fishing boat under the command of a godly skipper. They had been lying at their nets when a fierce gale struck. For three long days and nights they were at the mercy of the storm, which finally drove their ship ashore to perish with the loss of all hands. Their bodies were all recovered; the skipper found still lashed to the wheel. Three were buried in Orkney and the others taken back to their home port from which they had set sail days previously with high hopes of a successful fishing season. A large crowd gathered at the head of the brae overlooking the harbour as their bodies were carried up in total silence, by the light of a full moon. The entire village mourned the loss. However in the midst of grief there was comfort that they were absent from the body, but present with the Lord. It has been said that they had all put their trust in the Lord Jesus as their Saviour.

Today although boats and equipment are more modern, communications and rescue resources speedier, boats and men are still lost at sea. Life is still as uncertain as ever and souls can be ushered into eternity in a moment of time. This should cause each one of us to think of our eternal destiny, for we all have to meet God either in our sins or washed in the blood of Jesus, shed on Calvary for poor, hell-deserving sinners. Those who have believed in Jesus, have no fear of death and are filled with peace and joy in believing on Him. The question is—If Jesus called, would you be ready?

35

The Master of the Sea

' A ND ON THAT DAY, when evening was come, he says
to them, "Let us go over to the other side": and
having sent away the crowd, they take him with them, as
he was, in the ship. But other ships also were with him.
And there comes a violent gust of wind, and the waves
beat into the ship, so that it already filled. And he was in
the stern sleeping on the cushion. And they awake him up
and say to him, "Teacher, dost thou not care that we are
perishing?" And awaking up he rebuked the wind, and
said to the sea, "Silence; be mute". And the wind fell, and
there was a great calm. And he said to them, "Why are ye
thus fearful? How is it ye have not faith?" And they feared
with great fear, and said one to another, "Who then is
this, that even the wind and the sea obey him?" ' (Mark
4:35–41).

*'Thus saith the Lord, which maketh a way in the sea and a
path in the mighty waters'* (Isaiah 43:16).

36

Safe into Harbour

A S WE STOOD and gazed at the strongly-built boat fastened to the jetty in the old fishing town, we thought what a picture it was of the Christian mariner sailing o'er life's rugged ocean.

Storms all passed, dangers all behind, perils of the ocean all passed; she is safely landed in the harbour at last. So all who have Jesus as their Saviour and pilot will be landed safe on the heavenly shore.

Thank God, I shall be there; will you?

H.Y.P.

37

'Haven of Rest'

'I've anchored my soul in the haven of rest'

THE WIND WAS GETTING UP, the night was dark and the forecast was of winds up to force 10 and we were eighty miles from Peterhead. I kept checking the chart all the way in, to see if we were making any progress. We eventually saw the lights of Peterhead and arrived in the harbour after a very, very rough passage. I remember looking back to the harbour walls and seeing the spray and sea coming over and saying to myself, 'I'm safe now'. A sense of relief and joy flooded over me.

How like the joy of a sinner when he accepts the Lord Jesus as his Saviour and feels the burdens of his sins removed and forgiven by the precious blood of Jesus; he knows he is safe from God's judgment, 'and when I see the blood, I will pass over you' (Exodus 12:13). Safe under the blood of Jesus. That stormy night I could point to the harbour wall and say, 'I'm safe', but I can also point to the Saviour and say, 'I'm safe because of Calvary's cross and the work the Lord Jesus did.'

> The sinner who believes is free,
> Can say the Saviour died for me,
> Can point to the atoning blood
> And say this made my peace with God.

Can you point to the atoning blood? Have you peace with God? You will no longer have any fear as to God's judgment and you will be able to say:

I've anchored my soul in the haven of rest
I'll sail the wild seas no more
The tempest may sweep o'er the wild, stormy deep
In Jesus I'm safe ever more.

'He bringeth them unto their desired haven' (Psalm 107:30).

G.M.

38

A New Life

M Y NAME IS Gordon Campbell. I was born in 1949 and have been a fisherman since I left school at fifteen. For twenty years of my life I was known for my wild living, drinking, gambling and so on.

I got married when I was twenty years old and for sixteen years my relationship with my wife was just convenience; I forgot all about my marriage vows—for better for worse, for richer for poorer; I was there for what I could get out of it and while I was pretending that things were alright, my inside was screaming for a peace I just could not find.

In October 1986 I gave my life to Jesus Christ; at that time I was not sure that I could give up my past way of life, but I soon discovered I no longer required my past way of living and that the only thing I had given up was my place in hell. I have now found peace in Jesus and I have a family life of love that just passes all understanding.

Gordon Campbell
El-Shaddai

39

The Fisherman's Change

'WHEN YOU CAME HERE I thought I was the best man in the village, and now I think I am the worst.' Such were the words spoken to a friend of mine a few years ago as he was leaving a Scottish fishing village. No one who knew William Thomson, the hearty young fisherman, would have called him a 'bad man'. On the contrary,

he was upright, sincere and conscientious; the change in his views regarding himself was effectively through hearing a gospel preaching in which he heard that good works can never take away sins, only the blood of Jesus.

William and his wife discovered that they had been trying to work out a righteousness of their own in which to appear before God. Next day, the evangelist had a conversation with him and found him completely broken down. 'I am all wrong,' he said. 'It has been all works with me and no faith.'

What a mercy he made this discovery! He learned that all his righteousnesses 'were as filthy rags' (Isaiah 64:6). By faith he gazed on that blessed One who was wounded for our transgressions and bruised for our iniquities and passed from death into life—from darkness into light.

40

The Gospel Ship

H ANGING ON THE WALL in the homes of many believers is the 'Gospel Ship', a print of a large old sailing ship with every mast, sail and flag written over with a text from the Bible. I would like to draw your attention to some of the texts in order that, like many before, you too may be attracted to the Lord Jesus by the simple messages of the Gospel Ship.

Destination

Often while on watch in the wheelhouse, the fishermen would see many different boats; there would be cargo boats, oil-tankers, oil-rig supply vessels, yachts and fishing boats amongst many others. Every boat would be coming from somewhere, and every one would have a destination, and the first thing that you would wonder when seeing another boat would be where it was going. The Gospel Ship, like every other ship, is going somewhere and it also has a destination. At the top of the mast in the stern the flag says, **'From Land of Gloom'**—'A day of darkness and of gloominess' (Joel 2:2). Dear friend, the Gospel Ship is about to depart this sin-weary world for its destination on the flag at the top of the foremost mast. **'To Glory'**—'...then shall ye also appear with him in glory' (Colossians 3:4). Alas, there are many in this world who try to get from Land of Gloom to Glory without paying attention to the cross on the flag at the top of the middle mast.

As a sinner you must have to do with Calvary, because it was there that the Lord Jesus Christ died and shed His precious blood, in order that through believing on Him you might have your sins forgiven.

Passengers

Can I ask you a question? Are you a passenger on the Gospel Ship? The text on the sail tells us that the passengers are to be found in 1 Timothy 1:15 'Christ Jesus came into the world to save sinners'; and the Captain of the ship is none other than the Lord Jesus: 'the captain of their salvation' (Hebrews 2:10). He is crying out for you to come on board. The Captain's cry is, 'Where art thou?' (Genesis 3:9). All are welcome on board. The invitation is extended to 'whosoever will' (Revelation 22:17).

Time of sailing

Dear friend, come on board quickly because the ship is due to sail at any time. Indeed, one of the largest, most prominent sails on the ship tells us that the time of sailing is imminent: 'Behold, now is the accepted time' (2 Corinthians 6:2).

Crew

Fishing is a hard, demanding job, and all the crew must work hard together, often facing perilous situations with quiet courage and determination, praying to God for help and strength. The crew on the Gospel Ship also work together, '... striving together for the faith of the gospel' (Philippians 1:27). Are you a member of the crew on the Gospel Ship, spreading the wonderful story of Jesus to sinners?

Many fishing boats nowadays have modern video plotters to plot their course over the sea; the Gospel Ship is a little old-fashioned and still uses a chart. The necessary chart for the Gospel Ship is found in 2 Timothy 3:16;

which although an old chart is ever new and applicable today.

Fare and accommodation

Perhaps you are wondering if a passage on the ship is too expensive, perhaps you are anxious as to whether the berths are full. Let me quote you some more of the texts from the sails. The **FARE** is '...and he that hath no money; come ye' (Isaiah 55:1); and there is plenty of **accommodation**: 'and yet there is room' (Luke 14:22). Once on board the Gospel Ship your berth is secure: 'Him that cometh unto me I will in no wise cast out' (John 6:37). So we know that once we have trusted in the Lord Jesus as our Saviour He will readily receive us and will never leave us.

WARNING

The sail in the stern of the Gospel Ship billows in the wind with a final appeal: **'Come thou, Come, Come Now'**. Dear reader, I appeal to you to accept the Lord Jesus as your Saviour and you will never need to fear the warning on one of the sails which says, 'He, that being often reproved hardeneth his neck, shall suddenly be destroyed, and without remedy' (Proverbs 29:1). **Beware**—'Because there is wrath, beware' (Job 36:18).

Come to Jesus NOW

Iain J. Mair

41

All is Well

I N THE YEAR 1866, a most touching incident occurred exposing the folly of infidelity and proving the reality that God is and that He is near to all that call upon Him.

The scene of this remarkable incident was the district round the coast of the Moray Firth of Scotland where the greater part of the population of its many fishing villages are engaged in the fishing industry.

From one of these villages a tiny craft, with its crew of seven, sped to the fishing ground. All seemed to be going well. The lines had been 'shot and hauled' again, and a fairly good yield having been secured, the men prepared for the homeward voyage. The sail was soon set and the little boat was being rapidly driven by a rising gale that had suddenly began to blow. Hearts became anxious as the wind increased in fury and mountainous waves threatened every moment the safety of their little barque. Suddenly a gust of wind and a huge wave turned the craft right over and the crew were struggling amid the angry billows, and endeavouring to cling to the keel of the upturned boat.

Fortunately, all got a hold, and in this way were enabled to keep their heads above the water. I mention at this point, that the crew was composed of five brothers (Willie, John, Jamie, Sandy and Joseph), a young lad called Jamie, and a man named Smith. The brothers were all Christians and when ashore delighted to speak of their Saviour both publicly and privately and thus spread abroad the glorious gospel.

Thus in their moments of peril they knew they had an unfailing resource in their God and Father who marks the sparrow's fall and cares for His own whether in trials at home or the perils of the ocean. Clinging with death-like grip to the keel, the seven experienced the care of the God of the ocean, the God in whom they had put their trust, as time and again the merciless waves threatened to wash them away to certain death. Again and again the boy Jamie was washed off by waves, to be caught by Sandy who was a powerful swimmer, and replaced upon the boat.

Suddenly, to the joy of all their hearts, a large boat was seen to be bearing down upon them at a rapid rate. It came so near that four of them were able to grasp it, but all attempts to make the skipper return for the others were in vain. Their own safety, and that of their craft, were a greater concern to them than the lives of the three men now left on the upturned boat to what seemed certain death.

Let us now return to them. They had keenly felt the boat passing them as they faced danger and death, but rejoiced in the fact that the others were saved. With hopes blasted, and strength failing fast, they had often to release their hold and grasp again. At last Jamie in utter weakness said, 'Sandy I'm dune, I canna haud on muckle longer.' They all felt that the end was near, and Sandy who was a good singer, raised his voice and sang:

What is this that steals across my frame? Is it death?
Which soon shall quench the vital flame—Is it death?
If this be death I soon shall be,
From every pain and sorrow free.
I shall the King of Glory see—All is well.

Hark, hark my Lord and Master calls me—All is well.
I come to see Thy face in glory—All is well.
Farewell my friends, adieu, adieu,
I can no longer stay with you,
The glittering crown appears on view—All is well.

Jamie was too weak and exhausted to sing but when Sandy was finished, Jamie repeated—

> Lord Jesus, I love Thee, I know Thou art mine,
> For me all the glory Thou didst resign;
> My gracious Redeemer, my Saviour art Thou,
> If ever I loved Thee, Lord Jesus, 'tis now.
> I love Thee because Thou hast first loved me,
> And purchased my pardon on Calvary's tree;
> I love Thee for wearing the thorns on Thy brow,
> If ever I loved Thee, Lord Jesus, 'tis now.

When Jamie had finished Sandy said, 'We might have a little devotion and prayer before we sink beneath the waves and go to be for ever with the Lord.' Thus Sandy lifted up his heart to God and praised Him as the One who had sought them in their sins and saved them through the death and resurrection of His dear Son, giving them pardon, peace and joy and the assurance that they were saved. To die was the richest gain to them. To be 'absent from the body was to be present with the Lord'. To depart was to be 'with Christ which is far better'.

While Sandy was thus engaged in prayer and praise, the boy Jamie suddenly cried—'Oh Uncle Sandy I'm nae saved.' Every moment was precious. Death was near and eternity without Christ was a grave reality and Sandy immediately told Jamie the sweet gospel story. 'Weel Jamie my laddie, ye hae the same chance as the dee'in thief,' he began. Continuing, he told of the thief who was dying in his sins on a cross by the side of Jesus. He, our Lord Jesus, on the centre cross, had gone there out of love and compassion for men and was about to die, 'the just for the unjust to bring us to God'. The dying thief cried as he turned to the suffering Saviour, 'Lord remember me when Thou comest in Thy Kingdom,' and the immediate reply from Jesus was, 'Today shalt thou be with me in Paradise.'

In this way Sandy encouraged the boy to put his trust in Jesus and accept Him as his Saviour.

Should he do so explained Sandy all three would go to heaven together. Lifting his heart to God he prayed earnestly for Jamie's salvation, finishing his requests with the appeal, 'Ye saved the dee'in thief, oh save the drooning laddie for Jesu's sake.' Never was prayer more quickly answered, for immediately the boy cried out, 'Oh Uncle Sandy, I'm saved, I'm saved: I've trusted Jesus and I know I'm saved.' Thus with tears of joy, and hearts full of gratitude, the upturned boat in the midst of the stormy gale became the scene of praise and thanksgivings to God for His great salvation.

The prayer-hearing, prayer-answering God, intervened again and sent along another fishing vessel, the crew of which, unaware of the peril of these now exhausted ones, had been guided to the spot. Soon they were re-united with the rest of the crew, and their loved ones at home. There was great rejoicing in the village over a great deliverance experienced at the hand of God, and above all, for another soul secured to praise and serve our Lord Jesus Christ who had done so much for him.

Reader—does not this true, thrilling narrative of life and death touch you? Does it not impress you with the fact that God is a great reality? He cares for you, loves you, and is interested at this very moment in your blessing? Death is a great reality which you cannot face unprepared. Jesus, the Son of God, has battled with death's forces and triumphed, that we might have our part in the victory and be enabled like Sandy to say 'All is well' in the very presence of its power. God is prepared even now to listen to your cry of need and offers you pardon, peace and eternal salvation on the ground of the death and resurrection of Jesus, but fleeting moments call for urgency. Listen to the sublime appeal: 'Seek ye the Lord while He may be found. Call ye upon Him while he is near. Let the wicked forsake His way, and the unrighteous man his thoughts:

and let him return unto the Lord and He will have mercy upon him, and to our God, for He will abundantly pardon' (Isaiah 55:6,7).

W. Findlay
Portknockie
Scotland

42

Love that Changed Me

DEAR READER, do not neglect your soul's salvation, 'for now is the accepted time, now is the day of salvation.' Tomorrow may be too late.

Denis was brought up in a Christian home and in his young years asked the Lord Jesus to be his Saviour. He left school and became a joiner and then after a few years left the joinery trade and went away to sea.

During his late teenage years Denis's love for his Saviour grew cold and the attraction of the world and all its passing pleasures took a hold of him, and when home from the sea, late nights out in the town in Peterhead became the thing.

About three years ago Denis realised his life was heading nowhere and finished with his past way of life and was restored to the joy of his Christianity by Jesus' love.

I was at the wedding of Denis and his wife, and for his speech he had made up a poem and when he read out the last three verses many of us were affected.

The love that changed me, it was from Jesus,
From sin and bondage His love it frees us,
For on the cross the Lord hung in pain
For you and me, took our suffering and shame.

He died not for the perfect, but for sinners to save,
On Calvary's cross His life as a ransom He gave,
On the third day triumphant from the grave he arose,
And conquered death and the power of His foes.

For Jesus, He can save the hardest heart,

And when He comes into your life, He'll never depart
As His blood it cleanses us from every sin,
You too can trust Jesus and have that peace within.

Author
Morning Star BCK 10

43

Will Your Anchor Hold?

W HEN THERE ARE A GROUP of us in a house together we
   quite often finish with a sing-song and one of the
popular hymns is 'Will your anchor hold?' I enjoy it
because it is wonderful to sing of having your anchor on
Jesus.

> Will your anchor hold in the storms of life,
> When the clouds unfold their wings of strife,
> When the strong tides lift and the cables strain,
> Will your anchor shift, or firm remain?
>
> *Chorus*
> We have an anchor that keeps the soul
> Steadfast and sure while the billows roll,
> Fastened to the rock which cannot move,
> Grounded firm and deep in the Saviour's love.
>
> It will surely hold in the floods of death,
> When the waters cold chill our latest breath,
> On the rising tide it can never fail,
> While our hopes abide within the veil.

'Which we have as anchor of the soul, both secure and firm, and
entering into that within the veil' (Hebrews 6:19).

   The anchor is used to hold the boat but it does not
always hold and remain secure. The anchor for the Christian is SECURE which means it holds and it is attached to
a rock; the rock is JESUS. It is FIRM—seas may swell,
winds may blow, storms may rage, but the anchor holds,
it is unmovable. It is WITHIN THE VEIL or inside the

harbour. The Christian, by faith in Christ, has an anchor in the heavenly harbour where he is safe for evermore. The wise man of Matthew 7 laid his anchor on the rock: 'On Christ the solid rock I stand.' The foolish man laid his anchor on the sand. Avoid the sandy foundations; they move around all the time. The sinner is never at peace and tries so many different things but has nothing to hold on to, and when death, trials and sufferings come, he has nothing SECURE. Oh, sinner confess Jesus Christ as your Lord and Saviour and you'll be able to sing:

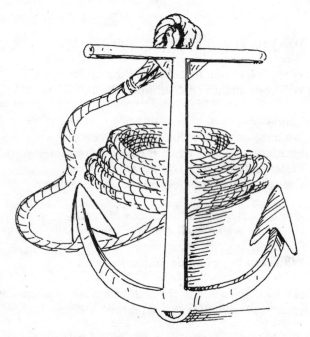

I can face the tempest shock, for I'm anchored to the rock
And His mighty arm my feeble strength upholds
Tho' the billows round me roll, there's a calm within my soul
Hallelujah! praise the Lord, my anchor holds.

G.M.

44

Under the Wave

O LD MARTHA BROWN stood at the door of her tiny cottage, looking anxiously up and down the long white road. The sun was burning hot with all the fierceness of a July noon-day. How her head ached with the heat of it! Her tired eyes swam with gazing at the hard white glare of the road in front of her.

Suddenly, she saw a blue clad figure slouching down the road towards her. She ran down the flagged path and flinging open the little gate, called in loving, thankful tones, 'Jimmie, Jimmie you've come at last.'

But her eyes were dim with ache and the glare of the noon-day; it was not until the man got closer that she saw that she had made a mistake. Although he was dressed in sailor's clothes, the face was to her the face of a stranger.

'Are you Mrs Brown?' he inquired.

'Yes, but what do you want of me?' she asked.

'My name is Peter Stone. I—I was,' he stammered, 'I am a shipmate of your son, Jim.'

The old woman's face lit up at the name.

'Ah I've heard tell of you,' she said, 'but where's my son Jimmie?'

'He—he, the ship struck a rock -an-,' Peter Stone could go no further and he turned from her.

'Ah!' A bitter little cry burst from her lips but clenching her hands she controlled herself. Drawing Peter inside the cottage, she made him tell her all. He told her how the ship, caught in a terrible storm, was hurled on to a cruel reef of rocks in the Pacific Ocean; and how of a crew of a hundred men, only twenty were saved. Jim Brown, the only son of his widowed mother, had drowned with the other eighty.

For some moments neither could speak. Then stifling her sobs Mrs Brown asked, 'Did you see my son die?'

'Yes,' he faltered.

'Tell me, how did he die?' she urged.

'Mrs Brown, I can't tell you.'

'Oh, but you must,' she replied, 'You must tell me. I know he died at peace with God for I have prayed so much for him.'

Again he refused but she persisted until at last in a broken voice Peter Stone said, 'He went down under the waves, cursing and swearing against God.'

Martha Brown shrank back as if she had been struck, then looking up she saw her favourite text over the fireplace: 'WITH GOD ALL THINGS ARE POSSIBLE'. Pointing to it she said, 'Even after what you have told me, I believe that God has saved my boy.'

The old lady's voice shook a little and tears stood in her blue eyes. She brushed them away and turning to Peter said with such faith in her voice that he never forgot the words, 'Then the Lord met him under the waves.'

Six months went by from the time when Peter Stone brought to Martha the news of her son's death. She lived all alone in her little cottage, tending her garden and communing with the Lord; still she prayed and believed that God in His love and mercy had come to her son in his last moments and taken him to be with Himself. For many years Jim had been a grief to his old mother, though he had loved her in his own rough way. He had been a hard drinker and brawler and openly scoffed at all religion. But all the time that faithful old saint of God prayed and trusted that Jim would some day be saved. Even after she had been told that he had been heard cursing and swearing as he slipped under the waves, she refused to give up hope.

On Christmas Eve she had a letter. She looked at the

writing on the envelope but it was blotted and smeared; she tore it open and scanned the half sheet of paper. The writing seemed to dance before her eyes, but with an effort she managed to read:

'Dear mother, I am alive and I am coming home today. Praise God! He has saved both my body and my soul, your loving son, Jimmie.'

Martha Brown laid the letter down on the table.

'Praise God!' she said, ' "WITH HIM ALL THINGS ARE POSSIBLE".'

That evening, while old Martha Brown sat alone in her cottage before the cosy fire, there came a knock at the door. Trembling she rose to open it, and there stood her sailor son. 'Oh Jimmie! At last my boy, my boy,' was her cry.

She saw a changed man, thinner and paler but with a new look on his face and a new light in his eyes. When the first greetings were over, Jim Brown told his mother how he came to be still alive. When almost drowned, he had clutched at a floating spar and clinging to it, had after many hours managed to swim to land. He had been found by a fisherman who carried him to his cottage. For weeks he had lain at the point of death and when he finally recovered, he was too weak to attempt the long journey home. Finally, after earning some money by fishing, he managed to work his way back.

Martha Brown hung on his words and when he had finished his story, she asked with eager voice, 'But Jimmie, how was it that you came to know Christ as your Saviour?'

'Mother,' he replied, 'the Lord met me under the waves'.

She started as she heard the very words that she herself had used.

He continued, 'I seemed to see all my sinful life and so I just cried, 'Lord save me!' And He did.

'HE IS ABLE TO SAVE THEM TO THE UTTERMOST THAT COME UNTO GOD BY HIM' (Hebrews 7:25).

45

'Nothing Shall be Impossible with God'

(Luke 1:37)

W E HAD A LAD who was an alcoholic. He was a fisher-man who used to cause all sorts of problems in one of the ports I worked in. Perhaps it is unfair to give his name, so we'll call him John. John had been a fisherman but he was now a severe, chronic alcoholic and had all the problems of homelessness and petty crimes that some-times go with alcoholism. We knew very well that he could cause trouble and create havoc if he came into the Mission; but one day I was called at the hospital to visit him. We chatted and I decided to take him into the Mis-sion Centre. For the first few days his language was ter-rible, his manners bad, and I must admit I was at the point of wondering what we could do for him and how we would cope with him.

One day we saw quite a dramatic change in his behaviour and his attitude towards the other residents, so much so that we inquired if he was all right. He told us that during the night he had met God in his room. On talking and praying with him there seemed a deep and complete change within his life and not only had we noticed this but some of the fishermen had also.

All he could speak about was what God had done for him. He certainly stopped his drinking and blaspheming and started to witness to those who visited him and any-body he came into contact with. Unfortunately, he died within a very short period. When we accept Christ as our

Saviour we become a 'new creature' and certainly this whole man's attitude was changed and he had become a new creature. We discovered that his mother had died broken-hearted praying for him. She was a Christian lady and so were some of his family, and they thought there was not much that they could do for him but pray for him. Thankfully their prayers were answered.

A. Slater J.P.
Senior Superintendent
R.N.M.D.S.F.

46

My Pilot

When hope and faith desert me
He holds me by the hand,
When sinking in life's stormy sea
He pulls me to the land.

When rocks jut from the water,
And winds they blow me near,
He changes my direction,
And I have nought to fear.

When danger lurks in the deep,
And I'm upset and scared,
He guides me to a safer zone,
A haven He's prepared.

When I'm up in Heaven,
It's Him I want to see,
And thank Him for the mercy
That He has shown to me.

Colin Mowat

47

Barometer

WHEN AT SEA if the dial of the barometer is pointing to 'fair' it means that it is going to be fine weather but if it is pointing to 'stormy' then it is time to pay attention because there is sure to be bad weather. I have read of instances in the olden days before shipping forecasts of those on the sea who saw the dial falling quickly to 'stormy' and made for shelter and some who didn't bother and thought it would be all right and perished.

I am glad that the dial of the barometer is pointing to 'fair' for me. With regard to my soul, 'it is well' (2 Kings 4:26) and I am bound for heaven where Jesus is and there 'he shall wipe away every tear from their eyes; and death shall not exist any more, nor grief, nor cry, nor distress shall exist any more, for the former things have passed away' (Revelation 21:25).

> There's a land that is fairer than day
> And by faith we can see it afar.

Indeed with the believer it is 'fair'.

For you sinner, the dial is between 'change' and 'stormy' telling you that you need a change in your life. 'Ye must be born anew' (John 3:3). You need Jesus in your life; you need a Saviour. There is judgment coming; there is wrath coming shortly for the sinner and that is why I'm pressing you to be saved now. 'Because there is wrath, beware lest it take thee away through chastisement: then a great ransom could not avail thee' (Job 36:18).

As with those on the sea in the old days, so it is with the people of this world. Some are paying heed to the barometer warning of Judgment and the need of a change in their life and are being saved; while others are paying no heed and are sinking into an eternity of woe and darkness in hell.

G.M.

48

'He Maketh the Storm a Calm'

THERE ARE TIMES at sea when I've seen a beautiful morning after a stormy night at sea. It is great to see the day break of a beautiful morning, it is just like the experience of the sinner after he accepts Jesus into his life. No longer tossed about under the storm of sin but all is calm in their life now, the dawning of a new life in Jesus; like the dawning of a beautiful morning after a storm at sea.

G.M.

49

'For God Speaketh Once, Yea Twice'

I AM A FISHERMAN and the boat on which we work involves a crew of twelve. Being employed in the fishing industry means that as crew members we are very closely knit together. This incident of which I am writing involves a journey by coach from Peterhead to Kyle of Loch Alsh on the west coast of Scotland. The reason for the journey was to join our ship as we were fishing off the west coast for mackerel.

We left Peterhead just after midnight on the Lord's day of November 3, 1980. The coach on which we travelled was not our usual one. As we were travelling along we were just past the Clunie Inn, about thirty miles from our destination when the coach left the road and four of the men were thrown out of the windows. Three of the men were slightly injured and the fourth was lying at the rear wheel of the bus. He was dead. As a result of this tragic death, one of the crew realised how easily it could have been him, and being without Christ he would have been lost eternally. He put his hand into my hand and said, 'I am saved now.' He had made a decision there and then to trust the Lord Jesus as his own Saviour. He had already had two accidents with his car before that. *'For God speaketh once, yea twice...'* (Job 33:14).

He was engaged to be married, so phoned home to his fiancée and she was saved on the following Lord's Day so it shows us that good can triumph out of these happenings.

The wife of the crew member who had been killed had

come to know the Lord just a fortnight before and he had been giving serious thought to his own salvation. Whoever reads this I plead with them not to leave things undecided. I did not get another opportunity to speak to that crew member but I trust that he had made his decision and trusted the Saviour before it was too late.

Peterhead Fisherman

Lie by till Morning

S OME YEARS AGO a large vessel called the 'Central America' ran aground, with the result that a hole was torn in her side and she began to leak. A signal of distress was immediately hoisted and another ship came alongside her.

'What is amiss?' asked the captain through the trumpet.

'We are in bad repair and are going down; lie by till morning' was the answer.

But the captain on board the rescue ship said, 'Let me take your passengers on board now.'

'Lie by till morning' was the message which came back.

For the third time, the captain of the rescue ship raised the trumpet to his lips and with an earnest appeal, called, 'You had better let me take your passengers on board now.'

'Lie by till morning,' was the reply which again sounded across the water.

About an hour and a half later, the lights of the vessel were missing: for suddenly, without any warning, she had heeled over and with scarcely a sound, she and all on board, had plunged into the depths of the ocean.

Oh, the danger in delay. Sinner, the opportunity is now, 'Behold now is the well accepted time' (2 Corinthians 6:2). By this time tomorrow many will have passed into eternity and if you are one of them and still in your sins you are destined for an eternity in *hell*. Fishing is such a dangerous job and you do not know what the next twenty-four hours hold for you.

DECIDE FOR CHRIST NOW AND DO NOT 'LIE BY TILL MORNING'.

G.M.

Saviour, Pilot Me

Jesus, Saviour, pilot me over life's tempestuous sea,
Unknown waves before me roll,
Hiding rocks and treacherous shoal
Chart and compass come from Thee
Jesus, Saviour pilot me.

How wonderful it is to know the Lord Jesus as your
Saviour, to know you've a friend who will be with you
forever.

52

Bill Duthie

B ILL WAS A YOUNG MAN of twenty-one years, and being very competent at everything on the boat one would have thought that Bill had no worries or cares. It only goes to prove that we can never estimate what is going on within a man's heart and mind. We were working long hours fishing and only managing to get about three hours' sleep out of the twenty-four.

All finished for another day, the fishing gear made ready for shooting the next morning, everyone made for bed smartly. I had the first watch in the wheelhouse—the ship just lying, the engine out of gear; when the door opened and in came Bill. He started asking a few questions about spiritual matters which I answered but also told him it was time he was getting some sleep as we would soon be starting again.

It was soon evident that Bill was serious to the point that sleep was far from his mind, and that he wanted to get right with God. He was very receptive to all that was being said; then he came to the important point—'I want to be saved,' he said. It was a great joy to see the young man coming to Christ in all his need. We thanked the Lord, then looking at the calendar, tore off the text because it was a 'new day'. It certainly was for Bill, the calendar read: 'A new heart also will I give you, and a new spirit will I put within you' (Ezekiel 36:26). What great encouragement right at the threshold of Christian experience.

To this day Bill says, 'It was just like Mark 4:37–39; there was a great storm and then after trusting Christ there was a great calm. The calendar text remains in his

Bible, 'A new heart also will I give you'; many years have passed by and we are still together.

Alex McLean
(Pathway)

53

Harbour Bell

W<small>E WERE NEARING</small> a dangerous coast and night was drawing nigh when suddenly a heavy fog settled down upon us and no light could be sighted and the pilot seemed anxious and troubled not knowing how soon we might be dashed to pieces on the hidden rocks along the shore. The whistle was being blown loud and long but no response was heard. The captain ordered the engines to be stopped and for some time we drifted about on the waves. Suddenly the pilot cried, 'Hark!' Far away in the distance we heard the welcome tone of the harbour bell which seemed to say, 'This way, this way'. Again the engines were started and, guided by the welcome sound we entered port in safety. 'The HARBOUR BELL' is ringing out from heaven tonight. 'This is the way walk ye in it' (Isaiah 30:21). It is ringing out to guide you, sinner, to refuge in trusting Jesus as your Saviour, refuge in the heavenly harbour from the coming storm: 'Jesus our deliverer from the coming wrath' (1 Thessalonians 1:10).

Extracted

54

The Controller of the Sea

'HITHERTO SHALT THOU COME and no further, and here shall thy proud waves be stayed' (Job 38:11).

'Jehovah, God of hosts, who is like unto thee, the strong Jah? And thy faithfulness is round about thee. Thou rulest the pride of the sea; when its waves arise, thou stillest them' (Psalm 89:8,9).

'When he imposed on the sea his decree that the waters should not pass his commandment' (Proverbs 8:29).

55

Safe Keeping

T HE WIND WAS STRONG from the SE and night time was
falling when we hauled up one Tuesday night ninety
miles north-east of Peterhead. The forecast was poor and
with the wind freshening we decided to 'dodge'.

For those of you reading this and not acquainted with
fishing terms, to 'dodge' means to put your boats head up
through the wind with your nets on board and wait for
the weather to fair. We set the watch and when I came up
after the midnight forecast to take my watch, it was a wild
night.

I was not long up in the wheelhouse when I saw the
white foam of a sea breaking down on us. It hit us with a
tremendous force and caused considerable damage to the
port side of the boat. About thirty feet of the boat was
damaged. When it hit us I looked to the stern of the boat
and could not see it for sea: the boat was awash. As I ran
out of the wheelhouse a verse in the Bible came to me:
'Fear not...for with me thou art in safe keeping.' Whatever the outcome I knew I was 'safe in the arms of Jesus'.

The crew came up immediately from the cabin thinking
a boat had hit us, but in fact it was the force of the sea.
After checking the damage, we 'dodged' until morning
and then headed for Peterhead for repairs.

How wonderful to know that in life we are in safe-
keeping and in death we shall not be alone. 'Yea, though I
walk through the valley of the shadow of death, I will fear
no evil: for thou art with me' (Psalm 23:4). How great are
the promises of Jesus, 'I will not leave thee, neither will I
forsake thee' (Hebrews 13:5). He will not leave us in life

nor forsake us in death. What a Saviour and friend we have in Jesus!

> I've found a friend, o such a friend
> So kind, and true, and tender!
> So wise a counsellor and guide,
> So mighty a defender!
> From Him who loves me now so well,
> What power my soul shall sever?
> Shall life or death, shall earth or hell?
> No! I am His for ever.

G.M.

56

The Gospel Compass

T HE LADY OPENING a harbour in north-east Scotland said, 'My prayer is: May God bless this harbour. May the boats as they go out and in, have His hand on the helm, so that all may be well with their precious crews and that not one may miss their entrance into that haven where no storms can ever come.'

Some decades earlier there had been a revival and many had been brought to know the Lord Jesus as their Saviour. A few years after the opening of the harbour, there was another and it has been said that there was not one boat that had not at least one Christian aboard; in the majority all were Christians. What a comfort this was to sorrowing relatives when tragedy struck! At that time on the walls of many of their homes, the Gospel Compass could be seen. At each point of the compass are gospel texts and assurances setting out God's plan of salvation. Between each point on a black background are warnings of neglecting this so great salvation. The text pointing north is the well known John 3:16, 'For God so loved the world that He gave His only begotten Son that whosoever believeth on Him should not perish, but have everlasting life.' This is the great theme of the gospel, telling of the wonderful provision from the very heart of God for needy sinners. At the centre of the compass are three circles, the inner bearing the words; 'God is Love', the great pivot on which the moral universe for God moves. The second, black, tells that sin entered the world and death by sin. The third, a red one, provides God's answer to the second; the blood of Jesus Christ His Son cleanseth us from all sin.

Directly above the north point on the yellow circle at

the circumference is the invitation 'Come'. Above this round the needle the words, 'And I, if I be lifted up will draw all to Me.' He is still seeking to draw and gather sin-stricken weary hearts to Himself. The yellow circle tells of the power of God to save and keep His own and that the end of all things will be for His glory.

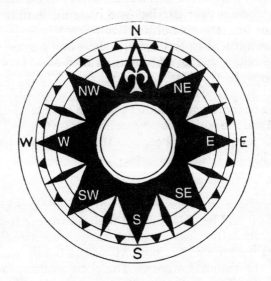

A compass is still necessary on ships despite sophisticated modern navigational aids. How much more vital is the Gospel Compass! Yet alas, how many are drifting carelessly to eternity on the sea of life making no provision for their precious, never dying souls. Do not be among them. While there is still time, heed the invitation, 'Come'.

Let the Gospel Compass be your guide.
Steer your course for eternity with Christ by it.

57

In Jesus I'm Safe Evermore

OVER A HUNDRED YEARS AGO, possibly in the early 1880s a sixteen-year-old lad was singing happily at his work on his father's fishing boat. Some time before, he had given his heart to the Lord Jesus and confessed Him as his Saviour. He loved to sing of Him and His precious love. Now, he was lustily singing:

> I've anchored my soul in the haven of rest,
> I'll sail the wide seas no more;
> The tempest may sweep o'er the wild stormy deep;
> In Jesus I'm safe evermore.

Just as he finished singing the last line—'In Jesus I'm safe evermore', the heavy sail swung round, knocking him overboard and he disappeared without trace. After a vain search, the father, sad at heart, turned the vessel round and headed back to the port where the family were staying for the summer months. The poor mother was grief-stricken. Although the family were filled with sorrow, their hearts were comforted that they sorrowed not as those who have no hope; the Word of God assuring them that He will bring with Him those who have fallen asleep through Jesus at the coming of the Lord Jesus for His own (1 Thessalonians 4:13–18).

What, dear reader, is your hope? If on the things of this life only, death ends all that. Have you fled for refuge to lay hold of the hope set before us, which we have as anchor of the soul, both secure and firm? Have you trusted in the finished work of Jesus on the cross and His precious shed blood? Oh! Lay hold of this blessed hope so that you too can sing, 'In Jesus I'm safe evermore'.

58

After Many Days

IN THE SPRING OF 1953 a young man of twenty-two years went to work as a hairdresser in Andrew M. Cordiner's barber shop for men only. His name was James Ritchie, but he was known affectionately to all his friends as 'Pim'. Very soon his cheery attractive manner endeared him to all, from the little boy with his first haircut to the old man with the hoary head. As it was in the shop so it was in the client's home if called there in time of illness. But, Pim knew not the Lord Jesus as his Saviour. Pim endeared himself to none more than to a young Christian lad of sixteen, a crew member of his father's boat the 'P.D. Quiet Waters'; his name was Robert Stephen. Robert loved to speak a word on behalf of his Lord and Master. So it was on Thursday 25th March 1954, Robert went to Andrew's shop and while getting his haircut, he asked Andrew, 'Do you ever speak to Pim about his soul?'

Andrew said that he did sometimes.

Again Robert asked, 'Is he saved yet?'

Andrew replied, 'No, not yet Robert, but ask him yourself.'

As soon as Robert was off the chair and standing in the middle of the shop floor putting on his woollen 'toorie' that most of the fisher-lads wore at that time, he said, 'Pim, does Andrew ever speak to you about your soul?'

Pim confessed, 'Sometimes Robert'.

Again Robert asked, 'Are you saved yet?'

Pim replied, 'No, not yet Robert!'

To that Robert answered, 'Well Pim, I hope next time I come back you will be able to tell me you are saved.'

On Sunday evening 28th March 1954, Robert along with

some other Christian lads were in a home, when Robert gave out that lovely hymn, 'Jesus Saviour Pilot Me'. In the early hours of Monday morning March 29th the 'Quiet Waters' left the harbour of Peterhead never to enter it again. For some of that crew their next port of call was 'The Glory' to be with Christ, and that was the case with Robert. A week passed before the people on shore realised what had happened and on Saturday 4th April the local fleet put to sea to search, only to find sufficient evidence that the 'Quiet Waters' would never again return. That was made known when the fleet returned to the harbour on Monday 6th April.

On Tuesday 7th April at dinner-time Pim and Andrew were going up the road together when Pim turned to Andrew and asked if he remembered what Robert had said. Pim then related all that Robert had said in the shop. Then Pim added, 'But, Andrew, he won't come back.'

Andrew said, 'That is true Pim, but where is he? And if it had been you, Pim, where would you have been?'

Pim said to Andrew, 'I know Andrew.' Pim was deeply touched but put off all further thought.

About a year later Andrew met Robert's mother, Mrs Stephen, who offered him some tracts entitled 'The Fisher Lad's Last Song'. Andrew asked for one for Pim which he gave him when he returned to the shop. Pim stood on that same shop floor (near the spot where Robert stood that Thursday) and read the tract through, then he took it and folded it up neatly and put it into his pocket book in the inside pocket of his jacket. For another four years he worked in that shop, gradually getting further away from any desire to be saved. He then left and went to Montrose, and was there for almost a year. He then returned to Peterhead where he started his own business and did well for a time. Then everything went wrong, his health also failed him and he had to go to London for an operation. He was in the Cottage Hospital getting built up for this, when Andrew went to see him taking with him some gospel tracts. In the middle of the bundle was one of 'The Fisher Lad's Last Song', which he had obtained from Mrs Stephen, one she had kept for herself yet willingly parted with, knowing the purpose for which it was intended. When Pim received them, he was looking through them and when he came to 'The Fisher Lad's Last Song', he said, 'Andrew, do you see that tract? If you open that drawer over there you will get my pocket book and in it there is a tract like that. You got it from Mrs Stephen to give to me and where I go it goes, and I have read it dozens of times. I'll never forget what Robert Stephen said to me. If only I had taken his advice what a difference it would have made.' But Pim was still unsaved. He went to London and had his operation, came back and seemed to recover, and was able to start work in another Christian's barber shop for a short time. He then started on his own again, but soon after took suddenly ill one Saturday and was rushed to Aberdeen Hospital. While there two ministers of the Gospel called to see him and in their presence he trusted Christ as his Saviour. He told all of the effect of those words of Robert Stephen over twelve years before, and also of the reading of that gospel tract that Mrs Stephen had sent him.

Not long after he was allowed home. Andrew went to see him and had to finish the testimony Pim was telling another Christian and had to verify as true the story about Robert Stephen's words. He showed the tract to all who went to see him, and was delighted to bear testimony to Mrs Stephen and Mrs Cordiner, Andrew's wife, of the Saviour he had found in Christ in the hospital bed in 1966. Soon he was baptised and received into fellowship in the Baptist Church in Peterhead. In November 1967 he passed Home to be with Christ, rejoicing in his sins forgiven, and in Christ as his Saviour.

Dear Reader, let me ask you: do you know the Lord Jesus as your Saviour? Do not depend on having twelve years as Pim had or count on having plenty of time. It is reckoned that the 'Quiet Waters' was lost on 31st March 1954 on the sixth day after Robert spoke to Pim. If Robert had not been ready, how long had he to prepare to meet God? Meet God you must, and remember 'Tomorrow's sun may never rise, to bless thy long deluded sight'. Oh! Sinner, now in time be wise, thou would'st be saved, why not now? 'Behold now is the accepted time, Behold now is the day of salvation' (2 Corinthians 6:2). Believe on the Lord Jesus Christ and thou shalt be saved (Acts 16:30,31).

59

The Best of Intentions

THERE ARE MANY PEOPLE in hell at this moment who one day intended to be saved. And you may intend waiting until you are older or whatever before you're saved. What folly! It brings to mind the story of a young skipper who had good intentions. The story is told by someone who spoke to him and who remembers the last evening he spent with him. He was quite willing to endorse every doctrine of our Christian faith—man's ruin, God's redemption and salvation through Jesus only; but when I asked if he had believed on, 'him who died, the just for the unjust to bring us to God', he frankly admitted that he had not.

Throughout our conversation he expressed, 'the best of intentions' and assured me of his purpose to get this great question settled before long. But when I reminded him that it is a solemn thing to trifle with God's word which declares, 'Behold, now is the well-accepted time; behold, now the day of salvation' (2 Corinthians 6:2), he tried to pass off my remarks with pleasant sayings, expressing himself satisfied that there was plenty of time to 'square the accounts'.

I remember his sailing from the harbour, in a boat that looked in good order. Not long after that he was drowned.

I never heard anything to assure me he had been saved. Jesus said, 'If ye believe not that I am he, ye shall die in your sins' (John 8:24).

The best of intentions, dear fisherman, will never get you to heaven. There has to be conversion: repentance towards God, and faith in our Lord Jesus Christ' (Acts 20:21).

60

Security

A FTER YOU HAVE COME through a stormy sea and into the harbour, you tie up the boat; you tie up your boat with a headrope and a sternrope and then you have a sense of security. The wind and sea may batter the harbour walls but you look at your ropes and know you are secure.

The sinner who accepts the Lord Jesus Christ as his Saviour is no longer tossed about in the stormy waves of sin but is now sheltered under the blood of Jesus and can look at the headrope and sternrope and see that his ropes are secure on 'Christ the solid rock' and that the impending storms of judgment can never touch a believer.

But alas, how many believers feel insecure—wondering if they really are safe—wondering whether in the end they maybe will be lost, still worried that maybe their sins are not all forgiven. Dear believer, the storm of judgment will never touch you because God has promised, 'and when I see the blood, I will pass over you' (Exodus 12:13); and your sins are gone forever, 'and the blood of Jesus Christ his Son cleanses us from all sin' (1 John 1:7).

Some believers who have thrown their ropes on to the 'solid rock' are still looking out over the harbour wall, worried about the storm outside, still feeling insecure, but I want to give you, if you are one of them, assurance of your security through the Word of God. I want you not to look at the storm outside the harbour but at your headrope and what it means, 'and I give them life eternal; and they shall never perish, and no one shall seize them out of my hand' (John 10:28) and your sternrope, 'Fear not, for I have redeemed thee...thou art mine' (Isaiah 43:1).

What words to hold on to, 'never perish' and instead of looking at the storm outside you look at the ropes on the 'solid rock' and with confidence in the security of the promises of Jesus, you know you, 'shall never be moved' (Psalm 15:5).

G.M.

61

Ready Now!

IN THE CITY OF LIVERPOOL, many years ago, on a cold, cloudy morning, the captain of a steamer was coming down the street on his way to the ship, when he noticed a poorly-clad, hungry little boy standing in front of a fine restaurant.

The captain placed his hand gently on the boy's shoulder and asked, 'What are you doing here, my little man?'

The boy with a piteous look, said, 'O sir, I was standing looking at the good things they have to eat in there.'

'Well,' said the Captain, 'I have but thirty minutes to spare before my steamer leaves; but, my little man, if you had on good clothes, a clean face, and your hair combed, I would take you into the restaurant and get you something to eat.' The little boy, with a look of love and gentleness, and with tears in his eyes at the Captain's kind words, brushed his hair with his hand and said, 'I am ready now.'

The Captain replied, 'Well, my little man, God bless you; come with me into the restaurant and you shall have something to eat.'

During the meal, in the course of conversation, the Captain learned the boy had been left motherless at the age of four and since then had never seen his father again. 'And who takes care of you?' inquired the Captain.

The boy with a look of calm resignation said: 'When mother was sick, just before she died, she told me Jesus would take care of me, and taught me how to pray and love Jesus.'

The Captain with tear-dimmed eyes, said, 'I have just a few more minutes before my steamer sails, and if you were dressed real well I would take you with me—you could wait on me.'

The boy looked and cried, 'O Captain, I am ready now.'

The Captain put his arm around the boy, saying, 'Come with me, my little man, and you will always be my boy.'

On reaching the ship the Captain introduced the boy to his men saying, 'He will wait on me, and his name is "Ready Now". He is always ready and you must not call him by any other name than "Ready Now".'

The Captain learned to love the child dearly. Shortly after being taken on board the little boy fell sick. The kind-hearted man took the lad in his arms and carried him to his berth to have medical attention from the ship's doctor. Although the doctor did his best it was evident the end was at hand.

The child continued to grow worse. One day the boy sent for the Captain whom he loved so dearly—death was near. The little boy, in a low, weak voice, said: 'O Captain, I do love you; you have been good to me. Now I am going to leave you and go where Jesus and Mother are. O Captain, I see my dear Mother, she is looking for me. Oh she looks so sweet and I see the angels and they sing so sweetly. Yes, Captain, I am going to be with Jesus. O Captain won't you open your heart to Jesus? Jesus loves you too, meet me in heaven. Captain won't you let Him save you and be a Christian?'

The Captain with deep emotion and trembling voice replied, 'I have been thinking about it and will attend to it soon.'

'But when?' again asked the boy. 'When will you be ready?'

'Well,' said the Captain, 'I will not put it off much longer.'

'O Captain, won't you let Jesus save you, when will you be ready?'

Weeping the Captain fell on his knees and cried: 'I am ready now—ready now.'

Afterwards some of the men came to the cabin and there they found him kneeling in prayer, the little boy's arms around his neck—the child cold in death's embrace; his pleadings had not been in vain, a faithful little worker to the end. The Captain on returning gave up his secular calling to serve the Lord Jesus in preaching the Gospel of the grace of God.

He told lost sinners of the Saviour, who, irrespective of state or standing, is willing to save at that moment—Whosoever will. 'Neither is there salvation in any other: for there is none other name under heaven given among men, whereby we must be saved' (Acts 4:12).

He pleaded with the careless and indifferent, because of the brevity of life and the certainty of eternity either in heaven or in hell. 'He that believeth on the Son hath everlasting life: and he that believeth not the Son shall not see life: but the wrath of God abideth on him' (John 3:36). 'Now is the accepted time' (2 Corinthians 6:2). Be ready! Ready Now!!

> Soon will the season of rescue be o'er,
> Soon will you drift to eternity's shore,
> Haste then, O sinner! no time for delay,
> But take now the Lifeline and be saved today.
>   SELECTED.

Alex Stewart
Hopeman

62

Saved at the End

T HIS IS THE TESTIMONY of Bill Sutherland, better known
as 'Nelts Bill of Findochty'. He was brought up in a
strict Christian home. He worked hard as a fisherman,
spending most of his time as a skipper working from
Aberdeen.

One night while he was at sea in a violent storm, he
struggled all night to save his crew and his boat. We can
only imagine what it could have been like, tossing about
in those conditions with mountainous seas seeking to
drown them. When morning came he somehow blamed
God for trying to destroy them. This incident became a
stumbling block and a burden to him through his life,
something he felt the Lord would not forgive.

Being a widower the last seventeen years of his life, he
coped well on his own until cancer was diagnosed. After a
year he became seriously ill, and I understand that at that
time he was very near to death and could have been lost
then. A Christian friend from Peterhead, David Davidson
made a tape for him of Gospel hymns, one being 'the
haven of rest'.

> My soul in sad exile was out on life's sea
> So burdened with sin and distressed
> Till I heard a sweet voice saying
> Make Me your choice
> And I entered the haven of rest.

I am certain this is how God called him. He carried on
coping with the illness, often playing this tape when he
was well enough to listen. Then one Sunday I was greeted

with, 'I have made my peace with God'; he began to explain how he had asked one of his daughters how he could be sure God would forgive him. She led him to 1 John 1:9, 'If we confess our sins, he is faithful and just to forgive us our sins and to cleanse us from all unrighteousness'. What wonderful words of assurance!

The Lord was listening to an eighty-one year old father's prayer; the doors of welcome were wide open. God was ready to save him. This was a very precious time; it was a time of great joy and blessing and also a very emotional time.

The last words Bill Sutherland spoke were, 'O Lord, give me the power to sing precious redeemer'. On the last day his speech left him but I felt that by his hearing he was still able to know as I sang 'He shall gather, he shall gather bright gems for his kingdom'.

> The Lord lifted us above our grief,
> Instead of darkness, there was light,
> Instead of hurt, there was peace,
> Instead of grief, there was joy.

If you are reading this and you feel that you are too old to be saved, then think again because you are never too old to be saved. The Devil will say that you are too late but he would always try and make you put it off. By this time tomorrow it could be too late.

> O come to the Saviour, he patiently waits
> To save by his power divine,
> Come anchor your soul in the haven of rest,
> And say my beloved is mine.

Nancy Cowie

63

Miraculous Deliverance

W HILE WE WHO LIVE out our earthly lives in this day of
the dispensation of God's grace, do not normally
see the hand of God working in an amazing and mirac-
ulous manner in everyday events, and it seems that most
things fall out just according to the cause and effect of
natural circumstances, there are times that an over-ruling
God must intervene so that all things work out according
to His divine will and counsels. Such is the Scriptural
doctrine of predestination and no one held this truth more
tenaciously than the skipper of the vessel whose experience I am about to relate. He was often heard to say, 'We
know not what the future holds, but we know who holds
the future', or 'Not a single shaft can hit till the God of love
sees fit.' So it is that the children of God are often called to
go through the most severe trials of suffering, bereave-
ment and persecution, but are sustained by faith, while
the childlren of this world may be blessed by the most
fortunate prosperity and attribute it to their own abilities
and effort, forgetting Him to whom all things are due.
Therefore, we are not to suppose that this miracle was
brought about because there were Christian men
involved, and we can see by Scriptures such as Luke
21:16–18, that while even violent death may be the
believer's portion, it is life everlasting that is promised.

The 'Replenish' was what was known in her day as a
dual-purpose vessel; a term which today has become
somewhat obsolete: a boat which is designed for both
seine net and herring drift net fishing. She was built in
Fraserburgh in 1950 and was about seventy feet in length.
Her skipper and most of the crew were saved; that is, at a

certain time in their lives they had taken God at his word, received his Son by faith as Saviour and Lord, and together with Him become heirs of the grace of life, and from that time forward, they had shunned not to confess His name before all men. This sometimes took a certain form, which I will now try to describe.

After the Second World War, receiver/transmitter radios became, for the first time, the normal equipment of fishing vessels; a great boon in terms of safety and communication as far as fishermen were concerned, but also a great channel of interest and awareness to people ashore concerning fishing, as they could buy radios with a marine band quite easily. Not only the fishermen's families, but most homes in Shetland had them and constantly listened to the boats as they spoke to one another or sent messages ashore.

In the summer months when the Shetland herring fishing was in operation, it became the custom for many fishermen, after they had shot their nets and before they took their short repose before starting the toil of hauling (which was toil indeed), to sing over the air, hymns of praise. Not only Shetland fishermen, but those from every port in the north-east of Scotland, took part in turn in this singing which might last from about 8.00 pm until 10.00 pm. Some sang of the all-availing cross work of Christ, some of the precious blood once shed for sin forever, others, of the sinless walk of the Saviour whilst among men, or, his abiding presence in the life of every blood-bought believer, or, the joy of Christian service.

John Pottinger, Skipper of the 'Replenish' and his shipmate, Harry Laurenson, were among the foremost in this work for the Master. They often dedicated their hymns to the elderly saints whom they knew were listening as they sang of the glories of the fuller life to come in that land that is fairer than day, and the joy of the Father's house; or to someone who might be listening who had not yet come to faith in Christ and was cast down in the shadows of daily care. They sang of the One who could lead them to the sunshine of light and love.

There is no doubt about the spiritual uplift that this singing gave to people both in the boats and especially ashore, as the novel concept of mens' voices being heard far across the water praising God, lifted redeemed hearts heavenward in soul-refreshing joy, and many still speak of those days as a blessed time that has passed. And pass it had to in these more modern days of speed and crowded radio channels.

John Pottinger and Harry Laurenson, along with most of the others, have passed also into the presence of the Lord they loved and served; whose faith follow. They now sing the praise of the Lamb once slain who sits upon the throne, and gaze with rapture upon the glories of the face once marred and smitten.

On the first Monday of December 1957, the 'Replenish' left her home port in Burra Isle, Shetland, for the fishing ground to the north-west of the islands. The wind was mostly light from northerly, but stronger in the occasional wintry showers. As they drew away from the land, the sea rose considerably and grew more turbulent with a heavy north-west swell. Long before daybreak, the sky became overcast and the darkness deepened. All hands turned out as it was obvious that they would soon have to make decisions about whether the weather would allow fishing or not. Other skippers started coming on the air, consulting each other about the weather conditions as they neared the fishing grounds. They would have to make up their minds by daylight.

When daylight did break, there was no doubt in anyone's mind. The wind rose rapidly from the NNW, accompanied by a blizzard of snow and the rising sea was strengthening to great breaking lumps of water. Every boat was now making for a safe harbour as best it could. The 'Replenish' was brought before the wind and was running a S x E course. With the engine governor to hand in the wheelhouse to keep the boat at the most manageable speed, the skipper kept the course. The mate who had kept the steering watch all morning was turned in. The rest were getting some warmth in the galley from the bitter cold. From the soundings, the skipper knew they were now crossing the Ve Skerry ground—tidal and treacherous in these conditions. No eye could see the breakers for the driving snow.

Suddenly, they felt her surge ahead before the oncoming sea. The skipper fought for control but she broached to and ran in broadside before the great wall of water which broke upon her and overwhelmed in its awful power, in the twinkling of an eye. Everything went before the great crash of the sea as she went over. Everything movable along with the ropes and net, the lashings of the small boat burst and it went too! But worse, the whole galley and most of the wheelhouse—of wooden construction at that time—along with all the men went also, into the raging sea. The mate alone was not washed off, but he was trapped in his bunk with the cabin table jammed tight on top of him and the sea cascading down the hatch.

But then the hand of God began to work in the situation, and the boat did not founder. As the skipper was being swept away, his hands found a grip of the top rail. With the boat still tearing through the sea, and with the resistance of a man's body towed through water, there was no other logical outcome but that even should that grip not break, it would be enough to tear the arms from the sockets. But human feebleness is God's opportunity, and the skipper not only kept his hold but gained the deck. Although almost all the deckhousing had been carried away, the clutch control for disengaging the engine still stood intact upon a stump of wood. He immediately went to this and took the engine out of gear. Although the ropes were hanging from the boat like tendrils, and the net was trailing about the stern, the propeller kept completely clear.

The boat by then had travelled some distance from the occurrence, before she could be brought up, and what of the five men in the water? The small boat remained afloat but deeply waterlogged, only the buoyancy tanks keeping her up, all oars and other equipment was gone. But, heaven had decreed that no lives should be lost that day and into this frail ark of refuge, a little boat no more than fourteen feet, came every one of the distressed men, with no very clear recollection of how it came about. But they were helpless and in the greatest peril, for a boat such as this would be almost overloaded in a calm sea, let alone among the billows of that tempestuous day.

Suddenly the 'Replenish', whom they thought to be no more, appeared for an instant while they were on the crest of a wave and disappeared again. What distance divided them, no one could judge, but the men in the boat could do nothing to lessen it. Aboard the 'Replenish', the skipper, now joined by the mate, was trying to cut away the wreckage of ropes and other gear that was everywhere around the boat. They were even hanging in bights from the lifting derricks showing how far she had been over in the sea. But this was proving no easy task for exhausted men. The ropes were jammed and wound round numerous projections about the boat by the force of the sea, and they dared not engage the engine again until all was clear, for fear of fouling the screw. While at this work they also caught sight of the lifeboat with its occupants, for an instant, which caused them to re-double their efforts to get clear and get to them. But it was not to be by man's efforts. In a very short space of time, the two craft were alongside each other, so close in fact that one of the younger men actually sprang aboard unaided. Should the question arise as to how this incredulous situation came about, we can only answer with another question—'Is the arm of the Lord shortened that it cannot save?' and are not all things possible with Him? The precedent is found in John 6:21.

Very recently I spoke to one of the survivors; he who boarded when they came together. He was telling of the experience, and when he came to speak of this, you could see he would have offered an explanation, but couldn't. He smiled, almost laughed, and shaking his head, said 'they just seemed to draw together'. Then glancing heavenward, he pointed upward with the finger and said 'It must have been...Him.'

I rejoiced greatly at his simple and uncomplicated faith. 'Him'. No other description was needed. He, the eternal creator of heaven and earth and upholder of all things, who in due time came forth from the Father and was born of a woman and laid in a manger; He who for our sakes gave His back to the smiters, and hid not His face from shame and spitting, but was led out with the malefactors to be crucified, and went into death that we might live forever; whose blood is ever before God, the pledge of our salvation. His eye was upon them that day, and He covered them with the shadow of His wings, and held the storm and the wind in the hollow of His hand, for He had appointed that they should sing His praise once again in the land of the living. Neither is their calling without honour, for did he not from their ranks call the first to be his future apostles, and His only recorded command concerning earthly employment, 'Launch out into the deep, and let down your nets', that he might manifest unto them his divine power and Godhead glory.

So they who were snatched from the jaws of death came again into their own ship. They speedily finished the work of clearing, and tested the steering while some manned the pumps. Only then did they engage the engine, and took her off the wind again and bore away for Shetland. But what devastation! No compass, wireless or cooking stove, and below, an upheaval of ballast stones, batteries, oil drums, flooring, fittings and bedding. Still they had the heat of the engine to warm their frozen bodies and the wind had moderated a bit and the sea, a little subsided. Best of all the sky had cleared so they could get their bearings from the snow-clad hills to steer upon, and make the best of what daylight was left of the short winter day, for they had to make land before dark.

But He who had begun a good work for them that day brought it to a conclusion, and as in the language of the Psalmist, He brought them again to their desired haven. And as in that same Psalm, they had surely seen the works of the Lord, and His wonders in the deep.

Shetland Fisherman

64

What a Saviour we have Found

I WAS BROUGHT UP in the little fishing village of Whitehills in the north-east of Scotland, born on the 14th November 1945, into a good home where I never saw anything of drinking, smoking or bad language. We went to church every Sunday and also attended Sunday school as my father was an elder in the local church. As I grew up I had a spell of ill health with asthma in 1953. There was a bad storm in January and I was quite ill at the time and missed a lot of school. As the years went on I left school, and started to work in my father's fish business, but all my chums went away to sea. My cousin who lived just down the road from us was thinking of getting a boat and asked me if we could go together in partnership; by this time I was already at the sea anyway aboard the MB Illustrious.

We went ahead and built a new boat, fifty-three feet long under twenty-five tons as neither of us had a ticket. So there we were, two young lads, with a good crew and very keen. The boat was about nine months old when I was hauled overboard while we were shooting the ropes. At the time I was going steady with Lorna who I later married; her sister had been converted a few years before and was often asking us to go to the gospel meetings but I would not go although Lorna would have liked to.

A few months later we were at sea fishing eight hours' north of Fraserburgh getting big catches of dogfish. We had not long hauled the net, the weather was poor and we were heading for Fraserburgh with the boat full of fish when one of the crew, a young lad, James Brown went overboard. We turned the boat round and saw him swimming but before we got close to him, he had gone under and had disappeared. We all took off our caps and clung together and cried; it was an awful experience to come away into harbour and leave a close shipmate in the depths of the sea; it is something that I will never forget.

A few months after that we were asked again to go to the gospel meeting held in Cullen. The preachers were John Gordon and Sandy Stewart from Hopeman. They had been preaching in Cullen for twenty weeks.

Lorna's sister finally persuaded me to go. I will never forget it: I heard something that I had never heard before, *'Christ Jesus came into the world to save sinners'* (1 Timothy 1:15).

I knew that I was a sinner in God's sight and that God had sent His Son the Lord Jesus into this world to die on Calvary, to shed His blood for sinners like me and to rise again on the third day.

When I heard this message I knew it was for me and I wanted to be saved and get right with God and have my sins forgiven. I thought I would have to do something or give something to get salvation, but it was by simply trusting in Christ's finished work on Calvary's cross and repenting, believing and trusting Him as my Saviour.

It was the last week of the gospel meetings and after the meeting one night we went down to Lorna's sister and at her fireside that evening on the 17 May 1969, in simple faith I trusted Christ as my Saviour. It was three days before my son Andrew was born. Lorna and myself thank God for his grace and mercy to us and for His keeping power.

WHAT A SAVIOUR WE HAVE FOUND!

Charles Findlay

65

Psalm 23

ALEC STEPHEN LEFT SCHOOL in Boddam to become a fisherman on his father's boat. Before they left for sea with the fishing fleet in the North Sea his father gave him a white card on which was printed the 23rd Psalm—in Scots. It had been written by John Moir, a blind poet who had lived at Banchory.

Alec promised he would keep it beside him. When things seemed black, if the going was very rough, he would read over the verses. Alec kept his promise. Voyage after voyage the Psalm went with him. When he entered the Royal Navy, the longing for home didn't seem quite so bad as he read over the verses.

Back home again, he rejoined the fishing fleet. One night at sea Alec became seriously ill. While he was being taken to hospital in Yarmouth he repeated to himself over and over again the Psalm he had come to love. When the chaplain of the fishing fleet, himself from a fishing community, visited him, Alec told him about the Psalm and asked if he would like to read it. When he'd finished reading it, Mr Wood said it was the loveliest thing he had ever read and asked if he could take a copy of it. He never ceased to wonder at the simple beauty a blind Scotsman brought to a lovely Psalm.

Alec carried the Psalm with him in his pocket book everywhere he went on the North Sea.

> Wha is my Shepherd weel I ken,
> The Lord Himsel' is **HE**,
> He leads me where the girse is green,
> An' burnies quaet that be.

I aften times wad gang astray,
An' wann'r far awa';
He fin's me oot, He pits me richt,
He brings me hame an' a.

Tho' I pass through the gruesome cleugh,
Fin' I ken He is near,
His muckle crook will me defen'
Sae I hae nocht to fear.

Ilk comfort whilk a sheep could need,
His thochtfu' care provides,
Though wolves and dogs may prowl aboot,
In safety He me hides.

His guidance and His mercy baith,
Nae doot will bide wi' me;
While faulded on the fields o' time,
Or o' eternity.

66

Almost Saved

Almost saved; and yet to sink
Over ruin's sudden brink
Almost saved, and yet to miss
An eternal throne of bliss.
Almost saved—yes see the door
Open on the unreached shore
Ne'er its happy threshold crossed
Almost saved is wholly lost.

O the peril of delay
Is not this salvation's day?
Is not this salvation's hour?
Christ, the Lord of love and power?
But tomorrow ne'er may be:
Sinner, to thy instant knee!
Christ is ready, Christ is nigh:
Touch him ere He passes by.

Almost saved, what woe so great
As to perish near the gate
Dropping at the threshold sweet?
Never of the feast to eat.
Perishing so near the board
Loaded by the eternal Lord!
O the shame, sad soul, of this—
Near to heaven, yet heaven to miss.

67

The Story of the 'Shegress'

T HE WEATHER was very stormy and the wind was blowing a gale as a trawler was trying to make headway
along the Yorkshire coast. She carried a full load of fish
and had eleven crew. Engine trouble had greatly ham-
pered her movements for a day or two, and during the
evening of September 24, 1935 she had been blown off her
course towards the treacherous rocks below the cliffs. The
skipper, who was a young man of twenty-eight years had
sent out wireless messages asking his position and had
received offers of help, which he declined. Not being well
acquainted with the east coast he did not realise how great
was his danger, and when told by wireless that he was in
a bad place, again refused offers of help. Suddenly, however, about eleven o'clock p.m. the wind veered a little
and made his danger greater than ever.

'Shegress, calling all stations' was suddenly heard over
the wireless and three lifeboats went out to render what
assistance they might. By this time, however, the storm
had increased to such violence, that not one of them could
get near to the wreck, which by then, had been dashed on
to the rocks. Men from the coastguard station on the cliff
brought a searchlight and life-saving apparatus to the
edge of the cliff, which at this point is four hundred feet
high. From there they could just see the men huddled
together in the wheelhouse and the great waves dashing
over the ship with tremendous fury. They fired their line
hoping to establish contact, but the wind which was due
east, blew it back every time. Until four o'clock in the
morning the sailors' cries for help could be heard; crying

when it was not humanly possible to bring them the help they needed.

Brave men in the lifeboats were risking their lives going through mountainous sea in a vain attempt to save them. Equally brave men on the cliff top were making every possible effort, in spite of the terrible danger of being hurled over into the sea. All to no avail.

When the dawn appeared at last, it was found that all hands had perished. Eleven precious souls launched into eternity—and why? In the first place, they did not realise how great their danger was. There are multitudes of people who are totally ignorant of the fact that every moment they stay away from Christ, thinking that all is well, they are in danger of being lost for ever. If still unsaved, think, as you continue to read this article, how terrible it will be to spend eternity away from God in the place of the lost.

The unfortunate men of my story had help and salvation offered them, but they thought they could save themselves. Perhaps, you too think that your own efforts will be quite sufficient for your salvation. Allow me to assure you, that there is only one who can save you and that one is **Jesus**. He not only braved the storm of judgment for you, but died on the cross and bore the penalty that you deserve; so that now by trusting Him alone and accepting Him as your personal Saviour, you can be fully saved.

68

Psalm 107

I REMEMBER my Granda who is now with the Lord telling me of a real experience he had at sea when he was standing in as skipper. They were fishing at Yarmouth at the time of the herring fishing when the Scottish boats used to go down for a few months in October/November.

They were out fishing when it came away a gale-force wind and a stormy sea got up. 'For he speaketh, and raiseth the stormy wind, which lifteth up the waves thereof: They mount up to the heavens, they go down to the depths...' (Psalm 107:25,26). They tied down their nets and headed for Yarmouth. He was very worried as he knew it would be bad at the entrance to the harbour as the sea was easterly and the way the tide was, would make it dangerous at the entrance; and with the responsibility for the safe keeping of the crew, he committed the boat and crew to a prayer-hearing God.

He stayed at the wheel all the way in and continued in prayer, 'Then they cry unto the Lord in their trouble' (verse 28). As he was approaching the entrance, the boat could not be seen for sea, but then as he came in to the entrance, the sea was calm and my Granda pointed to the table and said it was as flat as that, 'and he bringeth them out of their distresses; He maketh the storm a calm and the waves thereof are still' (28,29).

The boat continued up the river towards the harbour in Yarmouth and when he looked back to the entrance he couldn't see the boat astern of him for sea. 'They that go down to the sea in ships, that do business in great waters, These see the works of Jehovah, and his wonders in the deep' (23,24).

The experience brought praise and thanksgiving to God from my Granda. 'And they rejoice because they are quiet; and he bringeth them unto their desired haven. Let them give thanks unto Jehovah for his loving-kindness' (30,31).

G.M.

69

Saved from a Watery Grave

S HORTLY BEFORE MIDNIGHT on April 14, 1912, in the waters
of the Atlantic about 1,600 miles north-east of New
York, there occurred one of the greatest marine disasters
in all history. The giant steamship 'Titanic' the largest
vessel then afloat was making her maiden trip from Liverpool to New York, when she suddenly struck the under-
water shelf of an iceberg. Two hours later the ship sank,
sucking down all but seven hundred and six of her 2,300
passengers. In answer to frantic wireless calls the 'Car-
pathia' at last reached the spot and picked up survivors
from rafts and lifeboats.

Four years after the 'Titanic' went down a young Scotsman rose in a meeting in Hamilton, Canada, and said, 'I
am a survivor of the '"Titanic".' When I was drifting alone
on a spar on that awful night, the tide brought Mr John
Harper of Glasgow, also on a piece of wreck, near me.
'Man' he said, 'are you saved?'

'No,' I said, 'I am not.'

He replied, 'Believe on the Lord Jesus Christ and thou
shalt be saved.' The waves bore him away: but strange to
say, brought him back a little later and he said, 'Are you
saved now?'

'No,' I said, 'I cannot honestly say that I am.' He said
again, 'Believe on the Lord Jesus Christ and thou shalt be
saved', and shortly after he went down. There, alone in
the night and with two miles of water under me, I
believed.

Oh, dear reader whether young or old, may I ask you

the same personal question, 'Are you saved?' Those life-giving words of Acts 16:31 have been used to the eternal blessing of myriads of precious souls, whether read from the Bible or heard from the pulpit, they are the testimony of the Holy Spirit of God, and He can direct them to yourself as you read this magazine. Should they be used to your blessing, could I request that you write and let me know.

For with the heart man believeth unto righteousness; and with the mouth confession is made unto salvation' (Romans 10:10).

> When peace like a river attendeth my way
> When sorrows like sea billows roll
> Whatever my lot, Thou hast taught me to say
> It is well, it is well with my soul.

Extracted
Youthful Days

Fishers of Men

Fishers of men, fishers of men,
Jesus will make you fishers of men,
He in His service longs to employ
Those who would spread glad tidings of joy.

Fishers of men, fishers of men,
Joyous glad tidings, past human ken,
Sound out the message, tell far and wide
That for poor sinners, Jesus has died.

Jesus has died, Jesus has died,
He the Sin Bearer was crucified,
Bore in His body, burden of sin,
Back to His God, His creature He'd win.

Fishers of men, fishers of men,
Message of Jesus, tell it again,
Herald the Name of Jesus abroad,
Tell of the power of His precious blood.

Fishers of men, fishers of men,
Souls to be won for Jesus, who then
Life for the Master is willing to spend
Telling of Jesus, a Saviour for men?

Distress Message

The distress message comprises:

a. The distress signal MAYDAY
b. The name of the ship in distress
c. The particulars of the ship's position
d. The nature of the distress
e. The kind of assistance required
f. Any other information which might facilitate rescue operations

In Gospel terms:

a. The distress signal MAYDAY: 'And salvation is in none other, for neither is there another name under heaven which is given among men by which we must be saved' (Acts 4:12). The distress signal is **LORD JESUS**

b. The name of the ship in distress: .... (put your name in).

c. The ship's position particulars: drifting helplessly along to the rocks of eternity, drifting towards a Christless eternity in the lake of fire.

d. The nature of the distress: sinner, 'For all have sinned' (Romans 3:23).
'There is not a righteous man...all have gone out of the way' (Romans 3:10–12).

e. The kind of assistance required: a Saviour; 'Fear not, for behold I announce to you glad tidings of great joy, for today a

Saviour has been born to you...who is Christ the Lord'
(Luke 2:10,11).

f. Any other information which might facilitate rescue operations: have tried to obtain deliverance through my own
efforts, been baptised, been a regular at the place of worship
I attend; yet still drifting towards the rocks, towards hell.

If you cry to Jesus to be saved, Jesus will save you; no
one else can save you but the Lord Jesus, the one who laid
aside His heavenly glory and came to this earth and died
on a cross, shed His blood and rose again and now lives a
mighty victorious Saviour.

But, I want to warn you in relation to the distress
channel. Not every boat gets the opportunity to put out a
distress message. How many times have we heard of
boats gone missing without trace and without opportunity to put out a distress message. Things can happen so
suddenly at sea and if you put off being saved, of using
the distress channel to heaven you may be cut off, 'He that
being often reproved hardeneth his neck, shall suddenly
be destroyed and without remedy' (Proverbs 29:1).

G.M.

72

Accidentally Lost at Sea— Eternally Safe in Heaven!

O N TUESDAY, the 14th January 1992 at 8.45 a.m., a Mayday was sent out from the Lossiemouth fishing vessel 'Dayspring'—man overboard. The skipper and two
crewmen had been sleeping in their bunks, while the
mate, Jim Gault, was alone on watch, but when they
awoke Jim was gone.

The vessel had left Lossiemouth Harbour in the early
hours of Monday morning and steamed for eight hours in
the heart of the sea. Already they had two hauls and
fishing was quite good.

On the fateful day at 2 a.m., Jim with his brother Bill the
Skipper, discussed the course they would take before Bill
retired for a few hours' well-earned rest. The watch rota
should have been changed then, but Jim opted to take the
wheel. The weather was favourable and there was no
seeming cause for concern.

However, at approximately 8.30 a.m. one of the crewmen awoke and raised the alarm that Jim was missing.
After a fruitless search of the vessel the Mayday was sent.

Many people have asked how and why such tragedy
should happen. Jim was a comparatively young man,
forty-eight years old, and suddenly his life was cut off
without warning, but it could be conjecture on our part to
try to answer these questions, only God knows. We therefore have to bow and accept His sovereignty in such
circumstances.

The newspapers were given the announcement—'Acci-
dentally lost at sea'—yet Jim was eternally safe in Heaven.

As a boy of nine years, he had wakened from sleep with the sound of voices, for his sister Ann had told her Dad that she wanted to be saved. Jim listened while his Dad told Ann how she was a sinner and her sin would keep her out of God's Heaven, but the good news was that God had sent His Son, the Lord Jesus, to die on the cross of Calvary to bear the punishment for her sin. Jim realised that he too was a sinner and that Jesus had died for him. There and then he accepted the Lord Jesus as his own and personal Saviour. From that moment on Jim lived with the blessed assurance that one day Heaven would be his home.

That day finally dawned for Jim on the 14th January— he was lost at sea but eternally safe in Heaven. Absent from the body, at home with the Lord.

Dear reader have you this assurance?—For we all must needs die. When your time comes to leave this world, will you be save in heaven or be lost for all eternity? Make sure you trust Jim's Saviour and know with him the assurance that all will be well with your soul.

> My soul in sad exile was out on life's sea,
> So burdened with sin and distressed
> Till I heard a sweet voice saying, 'Make Me your choice',
> And I entered the 'Haven of Rest'.
>
> I've anchored my soul in the Haven of Rest,
> I'll sail the wide seas no more;
> The tempest may sweep over the wild, stormy deep
> In Jesus I'm safe evermore.

Ian Affleck

73

Great Joy

I WAS A FISHERMAN for over eight years prior to joining the
police force in November 1990. In January 1990 while I
was living in Elgin, something wonderful happened to me
that was to change my life completely.

Let me first tell you that I was married to Gwen, I had a
son Martyn aged four and another child on the way. I had
good health, a house, a good job, a car and yet I knew
something was missing in my life.

A close friend, Brian More had been a crewmate with
me for over three years aboard the fishing boat St. Kilda.
We'd worked, laughed and shared each other's company
at home and at sea. In November 1989 Brian became a
Christian, he'd been saved. Since that time our friendship
ended, I ridiculed him, laughed at him, mocked him and
completely ignored him.

One stormy night at sea, Brian was on watch with me
and as we dodged north of the Butt of Lewis I asked him
about what being a Christian meant. He began to tell me
about Jesus and His cruel death on the cross, His resurrection and our need to get right with God so that we may be
forgiven our sins.

Although I had always attended church, these words,
the good news, took on a new meaning. It was personal as
if God was speaking to me.

That night I went to my bunk and I couldn't sleep; not
because the boat was rolling about but because my heart
felt burdened with sin, guilt and shame; it was as if a huge
weight had been placed upon it.

Next day we landed our catch at Lochinver and Brian
and I went up to the Fisherman's Mission. I always

remember going to the door of the Mission and knocking at it and waiting for an answer. It would have been easy to turn back but I knew I had to get right with God.

The Superintendent also named Brian, explained what I needed to do to get right with God, and together we prayed. At 11.00 p.m. on January 24th, 1990 I prayed to God asking His forgiveness for my sins, trusting Him and believing Jesus died on that cruel cross, suffering and bearing my sins and shame; and also believing that Jesus after three days rose again so we may have eternal life. I asked the Lord to come and live in my heart as my personal Saviour. He did!

Words can never express the feeling in my heart that night and I praise the Lord for saving me.

When I told my wife she was quite hurt. Since being married we had done everything together but this was something you had to do alone; I had left home '**lost**' and returned home '**saved**'.

My first prayer on becoming a Christian was that God would save my wife. Three months later in the quietness of her bedroom she asked Jesus into her heart.

I could write a book about the changes and wonderful things Jesus has done for me, but I would like to share three of these.

First being a Christian does not exempt me from problems and difficulties, but what a privilege it is to bring them to the Lord in prayer and He answers them. The second is that before my wife and I were saved we thought we were in love; we were very close and enjoyed each other's company but let me say that until we'd experienced the love of Jesus we hadn't even begun to appreciate what love meant. And third is this, what a great joy it is to live knowing that when we die, as we all must, we have the glorious hope of spending eternity with Jesus.

Campbell Thomson

Homeward Bound

The voyage almost over,
The harbour lights I see,
And One who fully loves me
Waits there to welcome me.

Through many a storm and trial,
Through testings on the way,
I've proved His love most precious,
My comfort and my stay.

Thrice worthy is my Saviour
Of all my heart can give,
He proved His love so deeply,
He died that I might live.

He crossed the sea before me,
Triumphant reached the shore,
And there I soon shall see Him,
Be with Him evermore.

Soon shall my barque be anchored
And furled will be the sail;
Earth's trials soon be over,
I'll rest within the veil.

And there with Thee, Lord Jesus,
I'll dwell eternally,
My blissful occupation
In glory praising Thee.

D.F. Stott

75

Till We Meet Again

M Y BROTHER DAVID MORRISON, aged twenty-five years, died with his shipmates aboard the 'Acacia Wood' in 1978. He was a lad who enjoyed life to the full, rarely short of money and had reliable close friends. Life on the surface looked really good, but several months before he died his thoughts were not on the material gains of life.

He and I had to journey to Glasgow for a few days. Whilst there we had the opportunity to talk about many things. I was completely taken aback when he asked me if I believed in 'life after death'. At that point in time I was a regular church-goer but gave little thought to spiritual things.

His question made me feel very uncomfortable but I was interested to hear if he believed in it. He went on to explain to me that he had come to believe; I reminded him that he had a lot of living to do and advised him to leave such things alone.

He was drowned a few months later.

After our conversation I became aware that I had been unable to read him at all. He'd had such a look of peace and quietness about him that I felt totally separated from him.

Being a Christian now myself, I realise that during those few months he had been awakened spiritually. I was later told by our family minister that he had been reading the Bible regularly and believed in the power of prayer.

This knowledge eventually gave me a great sense of peace regarding his death. In Matthew 7 Jesus tells us, 'Ask, and it shall be given you; seek, and ye shall find; knock, and it shall be opened unto you.'

Elma Wilkins

How A Skipper was Saved after many Days

P_____ was skipper of a steam drifter and young P_____ as we called him, had just lately lost a child and was greatly upset by it; no doubt God was speaking to him. P_____ had three other brothers on board; J_____ was a Christian and there was also another Christian on board, R_____, that made three altogether who owned the Lord out of a crew of ten.

On a trip home, young P_____ asked me into his house on the Lord's Day evening after the gospel meeting, where his wife was seated by the fire; he gave me a chair and then sat down himself and said, 'I would like to be good living and so would Kate.'

'Yes I would, but don't know how to be' replied Kate, his wife.

I tried to point out that salvation was not by good works, but by owning that we are sinners and in need of a Saviour. We turned to the Scriptures together but got no light; so I turned in prayer to the Lord but with no apparent result, and as we were leaving early on the morrow I went home. It was impressed upon me to send a copy of *Safety, Certainty and Enjoyment* to young P_____'s wife through the post anonymously, so left this for my wife to do. This was used of the Lord to bring light into Kate's soul.

The skipper on the next trip was telling us of his wife's conversion and he said, 'I said to her, Kate, what have you got that you hadn't got before?'

'I've got peace' was her reply.

He thought that was not enough and still remained a stranger to grace. He had been to the gospel meeting on the Lord's Day evening and Mr Gray of Grangemouth had been preaching from Hebrews 2:3 *'How shall we escape, if we neglect so great salvation?'*

Next trip we were working in the North Atlantic off the west coast of the Orkney Islands and it blew a westerly gale, so after being hove-to for three days we ran for Pieriwell in Westray, where we were stopped over a Lord's Day. We were seated in the cabin when P____ came down and said that he had been listening to a preaching and the man was preaching from the same text as Mr Gray. He seemed greatly affected and was nearly on the point of deciding for Christ, but he put it off again.

When the gale abated we set out for sea again but there was still a heavy sea running. The skipper decided to shoot a few lines.

Next morning there was still a heavy swell and a good strong breeze. They shot the whole fleet of lines. They were hauling the lines when the skipper took off his oilskins to go down below, but he still had on his sea boots. He was helping to lower the mizzen sail when the yard swung over owing to the violent motion of the ship caused by the swell. It struck him and knocked him into the water. A lifebuoy was thrown overboard to him and the engines put on full speed astern, which raised me as I was off duty in my bunk, but knew there was something wrong as the engines usually go very slow when hauling lines.

When I sprang up on deck I saw the skipper swimming, trying to catch the lifebuoy, but the wind was blowing it away as fast as he could swim. The crew threw ropes quite close to him, but he did not see them as his back was to the ship and all the while he was going further away. He realised that he could not catch the lifebuoy and stopped swimming which had the effect of making him nearly disappear. He seemed for a few minutes to take no notice of anything (this was the time at which God was speaking to him, as he told us later). He then turned round and faced the ship. J____ S____ who had a line ready, threw it with all his might and the end just reached the skipper, who grasped it.

We soon had him alongside and on board where he fainted, but came round soon after; his teeth chattering with the cold he said, 'I knew something was to happen, I never slept a wink last night.' We got dry clothes on to him and put him into his bunk.

At dinner we got him to drink some coffee and he then started to speak, 'Did you see the time I was swimming for the lifebuoy? Well, my whole life came up before me and I saw my wife and children. While the water was gurgling in my ears, a voice said, "If ye neglect, if ye neglect so great salvation" and I said, "O Lord I will not neglect anymore" and I just turned round and the rope came into my hand. So I am to serve the Lord.'

The lines were hauled and we made for home. For the rest of the trip the skipper was very quiet and confined to his bunk but he said to me, 'I have got peace.'

On reaching home the news soon spread and was the topic of conversation among the crews of the rest of the boats, causing a widespread exercise, which continued through the Yarmouth Fishing and a great many were converted. All the crew aboard that boat were converted except one who later left and went aboard another boat as he could not stand hearing it all the time in conversation. He was later converted during the Yarmouth Fishing and came aboard every Lord's Day to rejoice with us.

77

Watching from the Shore

A SCOTTISH FISHING VESSEL was returning home after many days at sea. As they neared the shore, the sailors gazed eagerly toward the dock where a group of their loved ones had gathered. The skipper looked through his binoculars and identified some of them: 'I see Bill's Mary and there is Tom's Margaret, and David's Ann'. One man was disappointed because his wife was not there. With a heavy heart he left the boat and hurried home to his cottage. As he opened the door, his wife ran to meet him, saying, 'I have been waiting for you'.

With a gentle rebuke he replied, 'Yes, but the other men's wives were WATCHING for them.'

The Lord Jesus Christ is soon coming back to this earth. Are you watching for His return? He is coming back for His own, His Blood-bought people, who will be suddenly taken to be with Him. Will you be taken or left behind when Jesus comes? If you are saved and know Him as your own personal Saviour, then you will be taken when He comes. If you are not saved, you will be left behind with thousands who refused to allow Him to come into their hearts and lives.

'For the Lord Himself shall descend from Heaven with a shout, with the voice of the archangel, and with the trump of God: and the dead in Christ shall rise first. Then we which are alive and remain shall be caught up together with them in the clouds, to meet the Lord in the air: and so shall we ever be with the Lord' (1 Thessalonians 4:16,17).

He's coming soon, He's coming soon,
With joy we'll welcome His returning;
It may be morn, it may be night or noon,
We know He's coming soon!

78

Saved in a
Remarkable Place

Y OU DON'T HAVE TO BE in a church hall or meeting-room
to be saved, you can accept the Lord Jesus as your
Saviour anywhere. I was saved in my house and if you
were to go and ask a lot of Christians where they were
saved you would find a wide variety of places. I wonder
how many were saved in Peter's circumstances.

*And he saw two ships standing by the lake, but the fishermen,
having come down from them, were washing their nets. And
getting into one of the ships, which was Simon's, he asked him
to draw out a little from the land; and he sat down and taught
the crowds out of the ship. But when he ceased speaking, he
said to Simon, Draw out into the deep water and let down your
nets for a haul. And Simon answering said to him, Master,
having laboured through the whole night we have taken
nothing, but at thy word I will let down the net. And having
done this, they enclosed a great multitude of fishes. And their
net broke. And they beckoned to their partners who were in
the other ship to come and help them, and they came, and filled
both the ships, so that they were sinking. But Simon Peter
seeing it, fell at Jesus' knees, saying, Depart from me, for I am
a sinful man, Lord. For astonishment had laid hold on him, and
on all those who were with him, at the haul of fishes which
they had taken.*

If I saw a haul of fishes like Peter did, I would be
wondering if we would have enough boxes, ice and so on
and then I would be thinking of the market and prices;

but when you are dealing with your never-dying soul and the reality of eternity and being lost forever, a big haul and big shots of fish count for nothing. 'What shall it profit a man if he gain the whole world and suffer the loss of his soul' (Mark 8:36). If you are reading this in your bunk at sea, in the mess deck, at home or wherever you are and you are not saved, do not lay down this book without asking the Lord Jesus to be your Saviour.

G.M.

79

Lifeboat Refused

S OMETIME AGO in one of those tremendous gales which occasionally sweep the coast of Cornwall, a shipwreck occurred in the middle of the night. The signals of distress were heard and speedily answered by the gallant lifeboat crew at Penzance.

On reaching the wreck they witnessed a scene of unusual sadness. The captain of the ill-fated vessel, under the influence of liquor, was standing on board and would not enter the lifeboat, madly refusing to avail himself of the messenger of mercy sent to him in that moment of imminent danger. Not only did he refuse to enter the lifeboat himself but, drawing his revolver, threatened to shoot the first man who would dare to jump from the sinking wreck into the lifeboat. All the entreaties of the coastguard men were in vain. The drunken captain, bent on his own and his crew's destruction, obstinately refused to leave the wreck.

Six of the crew, perhaps under the influence of drink also, joined the captain in his foolish refusal to enter the boat.

At length, the commander of the lifeboat sadly and reluctantly ordered his men to row to shore with those of the ship's crew who had braved the captain's wrath. Far on in that dark night there came a lull in the storm and over the waters came the wailing cry, 'Lifeboat! Lifeboat!' Once more the gallant men pushed off toward the wreck but alas! It was too late. The wretched captain and his six men had sunk beneath the boiling surf. They had vainly called for the rejected lifeboat when it was too late.

'*How shall we escape, if we neglect so great salvation*' (Hebrews 2:3).

C.H. Mackintosh
Extracted

80

Wonderful Change

I WILL START MY TESTIMONY by going back to my Sunday school days when I was about five years up to about ten or twelve. I used to like listening to the gospel but later on in my teenage years like many of the young folk today I got into the wrong crowd. I was coming home from the sea with money that I could not handle and started going to pubs at seventeen years old and started drinking; being as young as I was I could not cope with it and started fighting. There was never a week went by but I was in a fight. It got to the stage when everyone was wanting to fight me and then I would pick up anything to defend myself and I ended up in prison on more than one occasion for months at a time and discovered it wasn't very nice. For the first week in prison your girlfriend and your chums look up to you as a hero, but that is soon forgotten.

I put the gospel out of my mind but I did not forget some of the things that I had heard.

When I left school I could not get away to the fishing quickly enough. My parents were against it even though my father had been at the fishing all his life. I decided to run away to Aberdeen and put my name down for the trawling school; that lasted three months and I passed, so I worked out of Aberdeen for two years. I went home occasionally and when my parents saw this, my father gave me all the encouragement to stick at it; he even got me a job in a couple of boats with him, but it did not work out. From then on I was working down in Grimsby and Shields for a time; on a lot of the boats I worked on over the years there was someone talking about what Christ did for them and I often thought that there was some truth in it, but that was as far as it went.

I got married and joined the fishing boat on which my father-in-law was skipper; when I joined the boat my wife's uncle was also aboard and another young lad like myself. The skipper and his brother had sailed together for thirty years and were both Christians and they often talked to James and myself about the gospel, but we hardly listened. One night while towing our nets the uncle was on watch and the rest of us were sleeping. When morning came we realised that he was missing and must be over the side. We searched along with other boats and helicopters all day until it became dark, but to no avail; he was gone, feared drowned.

We were all shattered when we turned the boat round to head for home, I just could not believe it: one moment we were drinking tea together and then he was gone. I could not begin to explain how I felt.

When we were steaming home we all had a good cry, especially the skipper who had just lost his brother. I remember him saying, 'Well William, he has gone home now and is in a better place' and he also told me the hardest thing he had ever done was turning the boat round and leaving his brother's body, though he was 'absent from the body present with the Lord'. Steaming ashore I was looking out of the wheelhouse windows into the dark night and I knew there was something missing in my life, an emptiness. When we arrived home the family were all talking about where he had gone, and that afternoon I went for a walk with Jim's son, Andrew, and he also spoke of where his dad had gone and I felt the Lord speaking to me again.

For three weeks after Jim was drowned I was confused and my mind was in a turmoil. I was heart-broken about Jim and I was longing for peace and hope in the midst of this tragedy; my whole inside was screaming out for something. We started to go back to the sea again and took on another two young lads on board. One was a Christian and we talked about the gospel all the time, and then one day he was preaching and I went along to hear him. That was when I asked the Lord Jesus to come into my life and be my Saviour; we went straight home after the meeting to tell the skipper; he was delighted at the news. As I started reading my Bible, I saw new things in life and what God wanted me to do. I got baptised and it was wonderful. We read in the Bible that Jesus died for us and rose again and is still alive today, and I know I will see Him again for He said I will come again. We have all our friends but Jesus is the best friend you can ever have. He is my best friend and my Saviour. All you have to do is open your heart's door and let Him in. He is waiting outside for you to call Him, so if there is someone reading this who has not yet trusted in Jesus, think what I have written. You don't have to be anywhere special, at home or at work, **Jesus is waiting for YOU** to invite Him in.

William Bain
(Dayspring INS 65)

81

He was Drowned;
I was Saved

THE MAGNIFICENT STEAMSHIP, Cyprian, left Liverpool on the 13th October 1881, bound for the Mediterranean. It was blowing a half gale at starting. However, in but a few hours, the wind increased to a hurricane and the decks began to be swept by heavy seas.

The ship received a lot of damage to the steering and the boiler-room, and in a disabled state the vessel laboured heavily until early next morning.

In heavy seas she drifted towards the Welsh coast and onto the rocks. Summoning all on to the bridge, the skipper told them it was now a case of every one for himself.

It happened that a runaway youth had secreted himself on board as a stowaway, unknown to any, before the ship had left Liverpool. Such passengers are rarely treated with favour by either master or mate. The young stowaway stood with white face on the deck terrified. 'Every one for himself,' again shouted the captain. Seizing lifebelts, oars, barrels, one after another the crew were obliged to leap from her deck and cast themselves overboard, many with but faint hope of reaching the shore.

At last there but remained upon the wreck the captain and the stowaway. The captain had just finished putting on his lifebelt and was about to jump into the sea as the others had done, when he saw nearby the white face of the terror-stricken boy, 'that little sinner of a stowaway' but a human being to be saved, if possible.

If any one had a right to his own lifebelt, it was the captain, and if any one deserved to go without it, it would be the young rascal beside him. Without pausing to consider whether deserving or undeserving, the captain took off his lifebelt and gave it to the stowaway and said, 'I can swim, you take this lifebelt, my boy'.

Overboard the lifebelted boy went, and after being dashed about by the waves he was rolled over on to the rocks, sadly bruised, but able to tell the story of his noble friend's heroism. Saved! Only just, but saved.

But what about the captain? Did he reach the coast too?

No never! He had struck out boldly, but the foaming surf was too much for him, and he sank—lost his life through saving another.

Every heart on shore was indeed moved as they heard the stowaway's account: 'he gave himself for me'.

'But' you say, 'this ragamuffin was no friend of the noble captain; all he deserved was a rope's end and yet the master died for him.

Such is the love of Jesus to you. No better than the stowaway: guilty, having sinned against the God of heaven, and yet Christ has died for you.

The Lord Jesus did not need to die, He could have gone back to heaven without dying, but it was out of love for *sinners* that Jesus died.

Hymn II

TRAVELLING ON THE SEA of life, we're homeward bound,
Drifting wrecks and struggling souls are all around,
But we do not fear the voyage, for we know
That the Saviour steers us as we onward go.

Chorus
We're homeward bound for glory...homeward bound for
    glory,
There we'll meet with loved ones gone before,
We're homeward bound for glory...homeward bound for
    glory,
All the storms of life will soon be o'er.

Jesus guides our storm-tossed barque across the seas,
He will bring us safely to the port of peace,
He's the pilot; He is standing at the helm,
And no angry winds or waves can overwhelm.

Come on board the gospel vessel, do not stay,
And we'll help you as we journey on the way,
Soon to harbour at our Father's blest abode,
We will worship in the City of our God.

The Lord is Coming

O VER ONE HUNDRED YEARS ago in Buckie, the fleet of
Fivies and Zulus (the types of fishing boats at that
time) put out to sea one night for fishing. The men were
like disciples of old; they had been out all night toiling
and had caught nothing. They were heading back in the
early hours of the morning, and to make matters worse,
not only had they caught nothing but the wind had gone
down and that meant that they had to row. During that
time there had been a great revival in the coastline with
many fishermen being saved. As they were rowing one of
the men started singing that hymn:

> Sweeping through the gates of the New Jerusalem
> Washed in the blood of the Lamb

and other members of the crew took it up and started
singing it, and as the other fishing boats were near it
wasn't long before in the stillness of the night, other boats
started singing as well.

The fishermen were still singing it as they came into the
harbour. On the harbour pier the fishermen's loved ones,
wives and sweethearts were waiting for them and they
started singing the same hymn:

> Sweeping through the gates of the New Jerusalem
> Washed in the blood of the Lamb.

As the fishermen wended their ways from the harbour
in Buckie to their homes, they came across an old Christian couple in their Sunday-best standing outside their

home. When the fishermen asked what they were doing out at that time in the morning, they replied, 'We have heard the angels singing and the Lord must have come'. This couple were waiting in their simple faith for the Lord to come.

'Behold, I come quickly' (Revelation 22:12).

84

Testimony

M Y NAME IS ALBERT SUTHERLAND and I am a living testimony to the saving grace of the Lord Jesus Christ.

I was born in 1946 into a Christian family, a twin, and
the youngest of ten children. I thank God for having
Christian parents; having a Christian upbringing gave me
a great start in life.

I gave my heart to the Lord one Sunday afternoon when
I was eleven years old, but it must have been an empty
profession because I drifted away from the Lord as I got
older, but God had His hand over me. I left school and
went aboard the 'Grateful' with my father and twin
brother. One day while fishing at the seine net, I was
catapulted over the side with the ropes; I can remember
my father's hand reaching out for me but the tide carried
me past the boat. At fifteen years of age I was facing death
by drowning, but God in His mercy preserved me. The
seine ropes were cut and the boat came round to pick me
up, very much at the end of my tether. 'For God speaketh
once, yea twice, yet man perceiveth it not' (Job 33:14). 'My
spirit shall not always strive with man' (Genesis 6:3).

As time went on I was still away from the Lord; I was
married in 1967 and in 1969 God took a part in my life
again. We were fishing out of Scrabster in the north east of
Scotland. Again my father—'Uncle Willie' as he was
known to people who came in contact with him, and my
twin Victor were there. We were working in the dark,
fishing for haddock, when on heaving the gear, one of the
trawl wires came foul of the rudder and unknown to us,
sheared three of the bolts that held the rudder in place. It
was a very bad forecast at midnight, a northerly gale, so

we decided to make for Scrabster which was about two hours' steaming time away. As we came along the coast we realised that the boat was being blown towards the land and would not steer properly. The steering wheel was all right and the Quadron down below still had the chains attached, but the rudder would not turn. The wind had turned into a howling gale by this time; the 'Star of Peace' which was a local boat, tried to come back to us but could not get through the wind and sea. God made provision once again. Another boat, the 'Star Divine' skippered by Jackie Ritchie—now an evangelist of the Gospel—came to help us. It was a terrible night as we lay broadside to the wind and sea, with the sea breaking right over the boat. Every rope had broken, the cleats had been pulled off, and we finished up with a warp wire fastened round the foremast and on to the winch. The lifeboat had been alerted by this time and was on its way to us.

I remember going down to the fore part of the boat to get lifejackets and when I went into the fo'c'sle, my father was down on his knees in prayer to his Saviour, and I believe that it is answer to that prayer that I can tell this story today.

The lifeboat came and towed us into Scrabster, in conditions that were atrocious. The lifeboat will always speak to me of salvation, but only physically because Christ Jesus is my 'lifeboat' spiritually. 'For God speaketh once, yea *twice*, yet man perceiveth it not' (Job 33:14).

My spiritual state was still the same until the 4th December 1979 when God struck me down aboard the boat again. The winch wire snapped and hit me on the back, breaking two ribs and puncturing my lung which resulted in five days in Aberdeen Royal Informary and thirteen weeks off work. During this time God really got to work by His Spirit and I could get no peace or rest. I went back to the sea at the end of February 1980 prawn fishing on the west coast. During this time I would waken in my bunk and rush up on deck, not knowing what was wrong with me. Gradually, I realised that God was dealing with me; I would be in the fish hold and find myself singing a chorus or a hymn from my childhood and that verse of Scripture in Job came into my mind.

I was a very troubled and confused man. I did not want to get saved because I was happy with the way things were; I had too many worldly friends who would not understand and the fear of man became a snare. God had other plans; He wanted me, unworthy sinner as I was and he was giving me no peace. In August 1980 there was a campaign taking place in Fraserburgh, 'Know Jesus, Know Life' with Dr Alistair Noble. On the Sunday, my brother James asked my wife, Jeannette and I to go along to the meeting. I came out the same way as I had gone in, unmoved and unsaved. I had left fishing and the family boat the week before as I wanted to get a job ashore. During the next week I managed to get a job working in the 'Taits' net factory. On the Saturday night, I went for my usual pint at the pub; with only half of my pint drunk, a conviction of sin came over me—I knew I was in the wrong place and, leaving my drink half-finished, I made my way home. My wife could not understand why I was home so early and sober into the bargain. I could not and would not explain it to her. That Sunday night was the last of the campaign and it was to be held in the Old Parish Church because it could seat about 1200 people. I decided to go that last night, so my wife and my daughter Alma, four years old, came along also.

John Gordon was to give his testimony. He was a policeman in Fraserburgh at the time of the 1953 Lifeboat Disaster and it was his sad task to go home and tell the news that the husband had been lost with six of the seven crew when the lifeboat went up the back of the South Pier after escorting in the fleet of yawls. The widow's words sunk into John's mind, 'My husband was prepared and so am I. He cannot come to me, but one day I will go to him.' Six years later John's five year old son died from leukemia and a Christian friend, Sandy Stewart, gave him a tract and the following words came to his eyes, 'I shall go to him, but he shall not return to me' (2 Samuel 12:23). Not long after this John came to a saving knowledge of the Saviour.

God was speaking to me while John was giving his testimony in such a way that I could not ignore it. I was involved with the lifeboat for two years after the station opened in 1978 after being closed due to the loss of our lifeboat in 1970 with only one survivor. This really touched me because I might have been there. I would have been in a Christless eternity if I had been aboard that lifeboat, but as it so happened I was away from home fishing. I took over as coxswain of the lifeboat in 1986. The meeting came to an end and the appeal was given, I used the excuse that Alma was asleep on my knee. The choir started singing, 'The king is Coming' and I knew if the King did come, I would be left behind; we went home, still unsaved but the Spirit was working on me and I was at the end of my tether but would not give in to God's pleading.

It was not until one-thirty in the morning, in the dark of my bedroom that I realised this could be my last chance, 'For God speaketh once, yea twice...'; and in my case three times. I thank God for a pleading Saviour. I got down on my knees at the side of my bed and asked God for His forgiveness. I had not prayed since I was a child, and the only prayer I could think of was, 'Come into my heart, into my heart Lord Jesus, come in today, come in to stay, come into my heart Lord Jesus.' The peace of God that passeth all understanding flooded into my mind and heart and I knew in that instant that I was saved. The peace was sublime and it was then at 1.30 a.m. in the morning of 25th August 1980, that I became a Child of God.

'Believe on the Lord Jesus Christ, and thou shalt be saved, and thy house' (Acts 16:31).

My wife, Jeanette, came to the Lord a few weeks later after the preaching of the scripture, *'And whosoever was not found written in the book of life was cast into the lake of fire'* (Revelation 20:15).

I had the privilege of praying with her and leading her to the throne of Grace and on to trust the Saviour.

Gary, our son, was saved a few years later, and Alma, a few years after that. The Lord has been good to us through the years and it has been a great privilege to serve Him, and we look to that day, when He will come back again for His own blood-bought people and we shall be forever with the Lord.

'And so shall we ever be with the Lord' (1 Thessalonians 4:17).

Albert Sutherland

85

What Makes a Man Ready to Die?

T HE ABOVE WORDS were addressed to the writer by a man who lay dying on board a fishing vessel, far from any hope of medical aid and with eternity staring him in the face.

One wonders if those who read this could answer this all important question. Perhaps the reader is saying that he has a long time to live; let me say that the man who asked the question was not an old man by any means. Death is no respecter of persons nor ages nor class, he visits the palace as well as the pauper's home. Money cannot bribe him nor can position in this life allow us to cheat him. All must bow to his edict, national or political distinction is of no avail when he gives the summons. One has met him at Calvary, for the Lord has entered his domain and has carried captivity captive and He death by dying slew. He bowed His head in death as the only one who has power to dismiss His Spirit, so one can meet death in the strength of one who has overcome him, for He is the one Who has tasted death for everything; or else meet him without a hope to cheer the tomb.

The answer to the question asked is simply this, trust Christ as your Saviour and know assuredly that beyond all this hustle which men call life, there is joy of the Father's house, or, reject Christ and know the lake of fire, with all its attendant weeping and wailing, as your portion. The choice is yours, choose for eternity—heaven, or hell.

Not yet decided; time passes on;
Judgment is coming; life soon is gone:
Yes, soul tonight may be
Mercy's last call to thee;
Choose for Eternity—
    Heaven or Hell!

A. Jack